PASTORAL CARE
OF OLDER ADULTS

PASTORAL CARE OF OLDER ADULTS

Creative Pastoral Care and Counseling

Harold G. Koenig and Andrew J. Weaver

FORTRESS PRESS   MINNEAPOLIS

PASTORAL CARE OF OLDER ADULTS

Scripture taken from the New International Version of the Holy Bible, copyright © 1973, 1978, 1984 by the International Bible Society. Used by permission of Zondervan Publishing House. All rights reserved.

The "NIV" and "New International Version" trademarks are registered in the United States Patent and Trademark Office by the International Bible Society. Use of either trademark requires the permission of the International Bible Society.

Cover design: Brad Norr
Cover art: Copyright © 1998 PhotoDisc. Used by permission.

Library of Congress Cataloging-in-Publication Data
Koenig, Harold George.
     Pastoral care of older adults / Harold G. Koenig and Andrew J. Weaver.
          p.   cm. — (Creative pastoral care and counseling series)
     Includes bibliographical references and index.
     ISBN 0-8006-2964-7 (alk. paper)
     1. Church work with the aged.   2. Aged — Pastoral counseling of.
I. Weaver, Andrew J., 1947– . II. Title. III. Series.
BV4435.K64   1998
259'.3 — dc21   98-28755
                                                                            CIP

Manufactured in the U.S.A.   AF 1-2964

02   01   00   3   4   5   6   7   8   9   10

This book is dedicated to my father,
Harold E. Koenig, on his 80th birthday.
—H. K.

This book is dedicated to my teachers
Schubert M. Ogden and Albert C. Outler,
with gratitude.
—A. W.

CONTENTS

EDITOR'S FOREWORD

I'm not getting any younger. (Neither are you.) That is a truism we can depend on. But Americans as a group are also getting older. We're starting families later. We're having fewer children. We're living longer. These facts have numerous impacts on society—on education, arts, economics, politics, health, certainly on churches—that are only beginning to be felt.

The graying of churches in the United States brings with it an expanding need for ministry to older adults and their families. Virtually all congregations include older persons. Increasingly, pastors face a variety of traditional and unprecedented issues concerning the aged. Ministry to older adults has become so crucial that more and more congregations are hiring clergy specialists to serve their senior members.

In recent years, one of the more common problems I address in my counseling is adults who have trouble dealing with their aged parents. Harold Koenig and Andrew Weaver, in *Pastoral Care of Older Adults,* address not only the issues of ministry to older adults but also those of ministry to adult children as they wrestle with how to care for their aged parents.

Before writing the book, Koenig and Weaver surveyed clergy in order to discover the most common problems encountered in ministry to older adults; the answers to the study generated topics for their book. *Pastoral Care of Older Adults* presents ways in which aged adults can maintain their physical, mental, and spiritual health. It also addresses a number of common, specific problems that older adults encounter. Alzheimer's and related diseases are covered in one chapter. Another chapter suggests community resources available to older persons and their families, including nursing homes, which 45% of all individuals reaching the age of 65 will enter at one time or another. The book lists and gives telephone numbers of agencies that pastors can call upon to help older individuals.

Koenig and Weaver also elaborate on ways to help older persons cope with chronic illness, anxiety, depression, grieving, loneliness and isolation, and terminal illness—in themselves and among their friends. They give specific suggestions for enabling lonely, disabled, or dependent older adults to feel useful and needed at a time in their lives when many have given up the idea that they have any ministry or calling.

I believe you will find that *Pastoral Care of Older Adults* has much to offer your pastoral care, counseling, and teaching ministries. It is written in a clear and specific style. It offers ways in which pastors can effectively care for individuals as they enter the last years, months and days of their lives, and it reveals how the congregation, as the people of God, can offer care to older persons and their families.

HOWARD W. STONE

INTRODUCTION

In this book, we answer specific questions and concerns of pastors and religious caregivers about the health care of older adults. We have purposefully chosen not to present our agenda. Instead, we have asked clergy and religious caregivers to identify the kinds of information they need in order to better carry out their ministry to older adults, and then we have responded to those needs. We focus here on the fifteen most common questions that clergy want answers to in order to better meet the needs of older adults and their families.

To find out what type of information pastors need, we developed a questionnaire that asked about health concerns of older adults and their families and administered it to clergy and religious caregivers. First, we asked what types of spiritual, psychological, social, and physical health problems older adults and their families commonly sought help for from clergy. Second, we asked which of those areas clergy felt least comfortable with or least prepared to address. Third, we asked which areas pastors needed more information about. We then synthesized their responses, prioritizing and subdividing them into fifteen major questions that are addressed in separate chapters. These chapters cover a wide range of topics, from changes involved in normal aging, to pathological conditions like Alzheimer's disease and depression, to information about nursing home placement and end-of-life issues (living wills, life support, and so forth).

This book is unique in that we have surveyed the needs of clergy and religious caregivers to find out what they want to know and have then responded to their questions in a precise, comprehensive, and professional way. Our goal is to provide practical information and help for clergy and their staff involved in day-to-day work with older adults and families. We present this material in a simple, straightforward, well-organized format to facilitate use by busy pastors and religious caregivers. While we expect community pastors and ministerial staff to be the primary audience for this book, we hope it will also be attractive to students in preparation for the ministry, pastoral counselors, hospital chaplains, and lay persons working with older adults.

1

WHAT HEALTH CHANGES CAN BE EXPECTED WITH NORMAL AGING?

"They will still bear fruit in old age. . . ."
—Psalm 92:14, NIV

By the year 2025, the number of persons age 65 or over in the United States will increase by more than 100%, in Japan by 136%, and in Canada by 200% (Dean 1990). In Europe, there will be more than 100 million persons age 65 or over in the year 2020 (Jamison 1991). Persons in the U.S. who reach the age of 65 have an average remaining life expectancy of 17.4 years; those who reach the age of 75 can expect to live another 11.1 years; and 85-year-olds can expect to live another 6.2 years on average (National Center for Health Statistics 1993). Chronic health problems, many of which are treatable, are common in older adults. Among persons age 65 or over, approximately one-half have at least two chronic medical conditions (Guralnik et al. 1989). In a study of a random sample of persons age 65 or older, nearly 50% died within ten years of the start of the study (Myers 1990). How does one determine what is normal and what may be disease in older persons? Many normal changes of aging are similar to and may blend in with symptoms of treatable diseases. Let us examine the physical changes that occur in the major organ systems of the body as persons grow older.

THE BRAIN

The brain undergoes a number of changes with normal aging. There is a small decrease in brain weight and increase in space between the brain and the skull. There is also a gradual loss of

3

brain cells, which are not replaced, at a rate of about 1% per year after age 60. Because of the tremendous reserve capacity of the brain, this loss of cells associated with normal aging has few noticeable consequences. There are also chemical changes in the brain with aging that may cause mild slowing of movements and a somewhat Parkinson-like appearance in older adults—head bent forward, stiffening of posture, shorter steps. There are three major afflictions affecting the brain in older adults that may speed and add to the changes of normal aging: Alzheimer's disease, Parkinson's disease, and stroke. Alzheimer's disease may affect 25% to 47% of persons age 85 or older. Parkinson's disease and stroke each affect about 10% of persons over age 85. As many as two-thirds of persons age 85 or older have one of these three major afflictions that affect the brain.

Changes in the brain with normal aging result in some decline in memory that has been called "Age-Associated Memory Impairment." These memory changes are completely normal and expected. They do not progressively worsen or herald a disease process. Persons may have trouble remembering a friend's name or may go into the kitchen and forget why they went in there. These people, however, have no difficulty functioning in other aspects of their lives. They don't become confused about where they are or get lost while driving in familiar environments. They continue to be able to perform complex tasks like balancing their checkbooks, paying their bills, scheduling and keeping appointments, preparing meals, and so forth. The memory changes associated with normal aging become more noticeable after a person reaches the age of 75 or 80. They do not worsen rapidly, however, and never interfere to any great degree with a person's normal activities or relationships.

Changes in brain function with age also result in older adults needing more time to learn new tasks, but, given adequate time to do so, they are able to learn and retain information as well as younger persons can. Older adults may also need more time to remember things or to retrieve information from their memories. For example, they may not remember something immediately, but often it soon comes to them. Thus, there is some slowing down in memory and other mental processes with age but not to the degree that it interferes with a person's life, relationships, or work.

Changes in the brain and nervous system with normal aging may also cause some minor problems with balance, coordination, and reaction time. These normal changes, if worsened by disease or medications, can predispose the older person to falling or other accidents.

THE HEART AND PHYSICAL ENDURANCE

As persons grow older, their hearts become a bit stiffer and don't pump out quite as much blood with each contraction. Their heart rates also don't increase as quickly as when they were younger in order to compensate for a drop in blood pressure or adjust to exciting situations. None of these changes, in the absence of disease, causes any significant problems for the individual. They do not cause weakness, loss of energy, or tiredness. Most of the time, those complaints are due to treatable disease processes. While physical endurance (as exhibited by prolonged physical activity) may decline slightly, it does not do so to any great extent as long as the older person remains physically active and in shape. Many persons over age 60 and even some over age 75 or 80 can walk or run long distances and may be able to keep up with or surpass many younger persons—especially those who are out of shape. The heart has a tremendous reserve capacity that is never used. While this reserve may decrease with aging, there is still typically more than enough left to enable older adults to perform the usual tasks of living (and even some extraordinary ones) without difficulty.

SKIN, MUSCLES, AND SKELETAL SYSTEM

Because of a reduction in fatty tissue immediately under the skin, the skin becomes thinner with age and is more subject to tearing or bruising. It is not uncommon for older adults to notice they are bruising more easily, especially on arms and hands, or that their skin may seem thinner and tear with only mild trauma. Bruising may be worsened by the regular use of aspirin or other medications for arthritis and other health problems.

While there is a reduction of fat in the skin, there is an increase in total body fat and a reduction of muscle mass with age. Fat and fibrous tissue begin to replace muscle tissue, especially if muscles are not exercised. Again, because of the body's tremendous reserve capacity, these muscle changes cause few observable effects on strength or endurance, especially if muscles are used regularly. However, the old saying "if you don't use it, you'll lose it" is true regardless of age.

Changes also occur in the skeletal system with normal aging. There is a tendency for bones to become less dense and more brittle. This is especially true for women after they have gone through menopause. The hormone estrogen helps to keep calcium in the bones. For this reason, many doctors recommend that women who have undergone an early menopause receive estrogen replacement therapy. If too much calcium is lost from bones, a disease called osteoporosis results. In this condition, the bones become weak and fracture more easily even with mild trauma. The hunched over posture of many older women is due to compression fractures of some of the bones that make up their spinal columns. Regular exercise, supplemental use of calcium, and, for some women, estrogen therapy can help stop the development of osteoporosis. Estrogen therapy, however, also has some negative side effects (uterine cancer, breast cancer), and women taking this medicine should be carefully monitored by their doctors.

THE INTERNAL ORGANS

Changes in the gastrointestinal tract, liver, and kidney are common with increasing age. Ability to absorb food is slightly reduced, and the function of the colon slows down, predisposing older adults to constipation. Again, these normal changes with aging seldom cause any significant digestive problems. Prescription drugs or over-the-counter medications, however, may easily worsen normal changes from aging and result in problems like severe constipation or other digestive troubles (heartburn, ulcers, and so forth).

Changes in the liver may affect the way the body handles medications. Most drugs are broken down in the liver or changed there into their active forms. With aging, there is a reduction of blood flow to the liver, decrease in size of the liver, and decrease in the liver's capacity to break down drugs and other substances. While these changes have little effect (in the absence of liver damage caused by disease or alcohol), they can interfere with an older person's ability to tolerate certain medications, especially if the person is taking several different drugs all handled by the liver. The level of certain medications can build up to high, even toxic levels unless these changes are considered. When prescribed for older adults, the doses of most medications should be reduced by one-third to one-half the usual dose for younger persons. This is particularly true for drugs affecting the brain and nervous system, which may be unusually sensitive to their effects.

Likewise, kidney function changes with normal aging and can interfere with an older person's ability to rid the body of drugs eliminated by this route. Blood flow to the kidneys is reduced, making it necessary to adjust downward doses of medication that must be excreted by the kidneys. (The liver and kidneys often work together in getting rid of drugs or other substances ingested into the body.) This makes older adults more vulnerable to overmedication because the body cannot break down these chemicals in the liver and/or excrete them out of the body through the kidneys as well as when they were younger.

Problems with holding one's urine or stool (incontinence) are unrelated to kidney functioning and usually have to do with damage from childbirth, surgery, or disease. Changes to the nervous system due to disease may also cause problems with the ability to hold one's urine or stool. Incontinence always requires medical attention.

HEARING AND VISION

Normal aging brings some decline in hearing (sensorineural hearing loss) and vision (presbyopia). The decline in hearing is usually more prominent for higher-pitched sounds than lower-pitched sounds. For this reason, older adults may be able to hear and understand deeper male voices better than higher-pitched female voices. Distinguishing sounds and words may also be more difficult for older adults. These changes in hearing can make it more difficult for older adults to hear on the telephone and to understand speech, especially in a crowded room or other noisy environment. Many diseases and toxic effects from certain medications can add to normal declines in hearing, producing problems that may seriously interfere with communication. These hearing changes can often be corrected, but older persons need to be very careful in purchasing hearing aids. They may find themselves with an expensive apparatus that provides little useful improvement in hearing.

Changes in vision also occur with normal aging. The lens of the eye changes in composition, often requiring the use of corrective glasses or changes in prescription to compensate. Because of this, vision should be regularly checked by an optometrist. Difficulty with visual acuity only compounds difficulties with balance, depth perception, and judgment of distance, which can lead to falls and traffic accidents. Several afflictions affect the eyes in later life, including cataracts (dimming or haziness of vision), diabetes, stroke, and diseases of the lining of the back of the eye. Many of these can be treated with proper medical care.

PSYCHOLOGICAL AND SOCIAL CHANGES

Most persons experience little change in their personality or interests as they get older. Persons who were outgoing and social in young adulthood or middle age will likely continue to be so when they are older; those who were introverted or social recluses at a younger age tend to have these traits when they are older as well. Sometimes personality traits become more accentuated with age. In any case, older persons usually continue to enjoy the same things they enjoyed when they were younger. This applies to work interests, hobbies, recreational activities, family, and sexual activity.

Depression, sadness, loss of interest, or unusual withdrawal from social interaction do not occur with normal aging. These are symptoms of treatable illnesses common in later life. Sleep disturbances in older adults are also treatable. As persons grow older, they normally experience a reduction in deep sleep and have more frequent awakenings during the night. They also experience sleep phase advancement; in other words, elders will tend to go to bed earlier in the evening and wake up earlier in the morning. Nevertheless, older persons require the same amount of sleep as younger adults do (seven to eight hours per night) and, if they do not get it, will feel tired and fatigued during the day. Treatable sleep disorders (insomnia, hypersomnia, sleep apnea) are very common in later life and may lead to emotional and physical health problems (depression, high blood pressure, heart disease, and others).

Those wanting to know more about the normal physical, social, and psychological changes of aging should obtain a copy of *The American Geriatrics Society's Complete Guide to Aging and Health* (Williams 1995). This fast-reading book includes a section titled "How We Age," which provides a wealth of practical information about physical and mental changes that occur with aging. There is also a section, "Conditions That Affect Older People," which explains the different medical conditions that elders commonly experience and discusses how to differentiate normal aging from these conditions. Finally, the book includes an informative section that explains Medicaid (Title 19) and Medicare.

2

WHAT CAN OLDER ADULTS DO TO MAINTAIN THEIR PHYSICAL HEALTH?

"Do not be wise in your own eyes; fear the Lord and shun evil.
This will bring health to your body and nourishment to your bones."
—Proverbs 3:7-8, NIV

There are a number of things that persons can do to help maintain physical health and vigor as they age. As we learned in the last chapter, feeling weak and tired are not normal accompaniments of aging without disease. Nevertheless, if an older person stops using his or her body, it will tend to degenerate. For this reason, it is important for older persons to exercise regularly, eat a balanced and nutritious diet, take care to keep their weight down, and maintain regular sleep patterns at night and activity schedules during the day. Furthermore, because mind and spirit have such a profound influence on the physical body, it is essential to keep these areas fit and active as well. Avoidance of alcohol (beyond two or three drinks per week), smoking, over-the-counter medications, and any unnecessary prescription medication is also recommended, because all of these may contribute to worsening health with age. Remember, however, that neither exercise, nutrition, nor healthy living habits will guarantee physical health or the absence of medical problems, but they will certainly increase a person's chances for maintaining good physical health.

EXERCISE

It is important for all aging persons to involve themselves in a routine of regular exercise that is appropriate to their physical condition. The frail older person with multiple medical problems may only be able to walk a few steps around the house each day or perform range-of-motion exercises with his or her arms and legs if bed-bound. Range-of-motion exercises are sometimes easier when performed in a heated pool or bathtub. Water aerobics are an excellent way for the elder with health problems to stay fit. An older adult with fewer medical problems and less frailty can develop a daily or every-other-day ritual of walking around the block or, in bad weather, walking around in a mall or department store. Even walking back and forth for fifteen to thirty minutes daily inside the house provides exercise for the elder. Some elders may find that taking tai chi classes and practicing this in their homes will help maintain balance and flexibility. For the healthier older person with few medical problems, walking for longer distances, running, or swimming are excellent ways of stressing the cardiovascular system and building endurance.

If an older adult has allowed him- or herself to get out of shape, however, it is essential to gradually get back into an exercise regimen. Strenuous exercise that is done only infrequently can predispose the older adult to heart attacks, strokes, and other medical problems. A complete physical exam by a physician and a prescription for a safe type of exercise with gradual increases are strongly recommended, and, for some persons with health problems, essential. Even ten to fifteen minutes per day of physical activity that stresses the cardiovascular system (increasing heart rate and giving a sense of mild breathlessness) can be very beneficial.

NUTRITION

While many advertisements proclaim the rejuvenating, health-enhancing, and energy-increasing effects of different vitamins and other organic preparations, it is likely that these substances contribute very little to the physical health of older persons who eat a well-balanced diet including fresh fruit, unprocessed green leafy vegetables, and an adequate source of protein (fish, fowl, or beans). Taking additional dietary supplements, unless the person has a specific vitamin deficiency, does little good above and beyond a placebo effect. Many vitamin supplements, particularly if they are water-soluble, simply pass out of the body in the urine without being utilized. Fat-soluble vitamins, if taken in excess, may even cause health problems.

Having three regular meals per day is important for older adults because it provides a regular schedule that may facilitate digestive processes. Recent research has suggested that red meat consumption (beef or pork, in particular) may contribute to certain forms of intestinal cancer, and it has long been known to increase the cholesterol that contributes to the development of coronary artery disease, high blood pressure, and strokes. Interestingly, Seventh-Day Adventists, who avoid meat, have lower rates of cancer and premature death from any cause than do members of the general population. Maintaining an optimum weight for one's height and build is also important to avoid putting undue stress on the cardiovascular system or the musculoskeletal system. Optimum-weight charts are available in most pharmacies or doctors' offices.

HEALTH MAINTENANCE BEHAVIORS

Aging persons must also pay attention to keeping levels of cholesterol low and preventing or treating high blood pressure. While hereditary factors play a large role in both blood-cholesterol level and blood pressure, there are things that older persons can do to optimize these health determinants. Cholesterol comes in two forms: a good kind, HDL, and a bad kind, LDL. The good cholesterol protects against diseases of the blood vessels and heart, while the bad type contributes to them. In general, persons should try to keep their total cholesterol (HDL + LDL levels) under 200. Cholesterol can be reduced by adhering to a low-cholesterol diet (avoiding meat fat, shellfish, cheese and other dairy products), losing weight, and getting regular exercise. If this is not sufficient, then doctors may prescribe medications to lower cholesterol (although the side effects of these medicines are not always benign).

Blood pressure should be kept below 160 systolic (upper number) and 90 diastolic (lower number). This can often be accomplished by a low-salt diet, weight reduction, and decrease in life stress or worry through regular meditation or prayer.

Avoidance of excess alcohol, unnecessary prescription drugs, over-the-counter drugs, and smoking are all essential to maintaining good physical health. While moderate use of alcohol may be associated with less heart disease and higher HDL cholesterol, any more than two drinks per day can worsen memory impairment, interfere with balance and coordination, interfere with other medications taken, and may worsen or lead to new medical problems. As a person ages, his or her brain and central nervous system become increasingly susceptible to the effects of alcohol, and alcohol-related dementia is the third most common cause of memory impairment and confusion after Alzheimer's disease and multiple strokes.

Because of multiple medical and psychological problems, older adults are often taking many different prescription and nonprescription medications. Some of these medications may be unnecessary, may be interacting with each other, and may be contributing to difficulty with memory or to increased risk of falling or other injury. Only medications that are absolutely necessary should be taken. The older adult, however, should not decide on his or her own which medications are necessary or unnecessary. A physician with training and interest in the health problems of older adults should be consulted and, if results are not satisfactory, a second opinion obtained. While a number of elderly adults have anxiety disorders that require drugs, the most commonly overused drugs are those taken for anxiety or insomnia.

3

WHAT CAN OLDER ADULTS DO TO ACHIEVE AND MAINTAIN THEIR MENTAL HEALTH?

"For God hath not given us the spirit of fear; but of power, and of love, and of a sound mind."
—2 Timothy 1:7, KJV

While there are a number of things that aging persons can do to maintain physical health, changes in physical health often occur regardless of what a person does. With regard to maintaining mental health, however, there are many things that aging persons can do. In fact, one's mental health is largely in his or her own hands. Of course, memory disorders like Alzheimer's disease, thought disorders like schizophrenia, or other mental conditions largely determined by hereditary factors or biological diseases are not afflictions an aging person can control. In chapter 5, we will discuss what, if anything, persons can do to prevent memory problems in late life.

In general, aging persons can best maintain their mental health by staying socially active and involved, avoiding alcohol and drugs to cope with life's problems, and choosing to think and behave in healthy ways that reduce psychological stress.

BECOMING AND STAYING SOCIALLY ACTIVE

About thirty years ago, there was a popular theory among social scientists in the field of gerontology that normal aging was associated with a withdrawal from interaction with others and an increase in introversion. This became known as the disengagement theory of aging; in other words, it was thought normal for persons to disengage from social relationships and withdraw into themselves as they grew older. We know now that this theory was incorrect. Far from being exemplary of normal aging, it turns out that many older persons in these studies had treatable mental or physical health conditions (depression, dementia, and other diseases) that were not recognized.

Several years ago, activity theory replaced disengagement theory as a model for normal, healthy aging. This theory maintains, more understandably, that physical and mental activity, which fosters involvement in social relationships, increases the likelihood that aging persons will age successfully. Human beings are social creatures and require ongoing contact with others to remain mentally healthy, just as their bodies require nutrition to stay physically healthy.

AVOIDING ALCOHOL AND DRUGS

Just as physical health depends on avoidance of behaviors or habits that are destructive to the body, mental health requires that persons avoid substances that adversely affect their minds. These substances include alcohol, tranquilizers, and sleeping aids. The central nervous system and brain of an aging person become increasingly sensitive to the effects of these substances. In addition, because of physiological changes in the body with aging (decreased liver metabolism, decreased water-to-fat ratio), a given amount of ingested alcohol will result in a higher blood-alcohol level in an aging person than in a younger adult. Alcohol, minor tranquilizers (like Valium®), and narcotics taken for pain are all central nervous system depressants and, therefore, can cause or contribute to depression, fatigue, lethargy, and loss of interest. Whenever possible these drugs should be avoided.

Regular exercise and good sleep habits have also been associated with better mental health and increased energy in older adults.

HEALTHY WAYS OF THINKING AND BEHAVING

Because of heredity factors, negative experiences while growing up, or psychological traumas in adulthood, certain persons are more vulnerable to the development of depression or anxiety disorders when they must face major life stressors. Many emotional problems are preventable, however, and joy and life satisfaction may be increased by certain attitudes and behaviors. These attitudes and behaviors do not usually come naturally. In fact, the most natural response to many of the changes of aging (loss of loved ones, worsening health, declining finances, and so forth) is attitudes that generate feelings of hopelessness, despair, and desire to withdraw and give up. In order to counteract these negative attitudes and feelings, the influence of the Holy Spirit is beneficial.

In our estimation, a key to mental health in late life is thought, belief, and behavior that stems from faith in God. This is precisely what many in the Judeo-Christian tradition have been proclaiming for thousands of years as the key to spiritual growth and maturation. Studies show, however, that this is also the most powerful prescription for mental health as well as spiritual health. It is especially necessary as persons age and begin to lose their grasp on the things of this world that previously held their confidence. Solid scientific research is repeatedly demonstrating that trust and faith in God provides a mental stability that can weather losses and changes, which cannot be prevented as one ages (Koenig 1997). Even if chronically ill older persons are depressed and overwhelmed with their circumstances, when their religious faith is strong, studies show that they will recover more quickly than persons who do not have this source of strength (Koenig et al. 1998).

Aging is truly a time when coping resources—things that can help compensate for traumatic loss and return value and meaning to life—are seriously tested. Less resilient coping resources such as health, roles played in society, financial accomplishments, even personal relationships, begin to lose their usefulness as persons become chronically ill, dependent, and approach the end of their lives. It is during these circumstances that a relationship with God will become more and more important, partly because other things may lose their ability to comfort.

One of the best ways to maintain mental health as persons grow older is to invest energy and time into loving and serving God, and ministering to the needs of persons whose needs are greater. Bringing happiness to others, enhancing other persons' lives, and being generous with one's time and resources provides a mind-set that will bring fulfillment and mental stability to the aging person. In our opinion, this is one of the quickest and surest ways of achieving and maintaining emotional fulfillment and stability.

Staying mentally active by reading, engaging in a favorite hobby, or staying socially active does not assure emotional and mental stability when chronic illness strikes, vision becomes impaired, disability forces dependency on others, and relatives and friends die or relocate because of their own health problems. A person's faith, on the other hand, is a constant source of comfort, when he or she is alone, in the middle of the night, or in any other situation, circumstance, or time in life. Research indicates that faith is an important resource for well-being when stress is highest and circumstances are the dimmest (Koenig et al. 1992; Koenig et al. 1998).

Principles of modern psychology are not particularly useful for preventing emotional distress in response to real life stressors of the magnitude encountered by many older adults—the death of a spouse after fifty years of marriage, the sudden disability brought on by a stroke in someone previously self-sufficient, the need to sell one's house and possessions and move into a single room in a nursing home. After a time, even one's closest friends may stop coming to visit and stop providing emotional support in these situations. These are the types of stressors that many older adults must face, and this is when religious faith can often help people not to give up. Persons with strong religious faith have their emotional well-being built on a rock foundation that will not fall even under such trying circumstances. These assertions are based on solid, recent research repeatedly showing that well-being is higher and depression is lower among those persons with physical illness and functional disability who have a strong faith in God (Koenig 1997). If persons rely only on the goodwill of others or on their own psychological strength to sustain emotional well-being, they will be building their houses on sand, which will wash away when the storms and heavy rains of old age come along.

Obviously, centering one's life on God and devoting one's life to serve those in need are not easy tasks. There are pitfalls and road blocks that may at times discourage and dishearten even the strongest and most faithful individual, but the ultimate spiritual gains will bring long-term mental health consequences that far outweigh the effort. Someone once said that you cannot find happiness no matter how hard you search for it; you can only provide it to others, and, in doing so, you will experience it yourself. Older adults who are happiest are those generous souls who give of themselves to others, abandoning their own self-centered preoccupations. In a previous book, *A Gospel for the Mature Years,* we have provided aids to help middle-aged and older adults discover their gifts and use them to serve God through serving others in whatever circumstance they find themselves (Koenig et al. 1997).

> Lord, make me an instrument of your peace!
> Where there is hatred, let me sow love;
> Where there is injury, pardon;
> Where there is doubt, faith;
> Where there is despair, hope;
> Where there is sadness, joy.
> O Divine Master,
> Grant that I may not so much seek to be consoled as to console,
> To be understood as to understand,
> To be loved as to love;
> For it is in giving that we receive;
> It is in pardoning that we are pardoned;
> And it is in dying that we are born to eternal life.
> —PRAYER OF FRANCIS OF ASSISI

4

HOW CAN SPIRITUAL GROWTH BE FACILITATED IN LATER LIFE?

"But the fruit of the Spirit is love, joy, peace, patience, kindness, goodness, faithfulness. . . ."
—Galatians 5:22, NIV

As mental health professionals and persons of faith, we believe that facilitating spiritual growth is ultimately the most effective way of maintaining mental health, physical health, and vigor. We know the mind has an enormous influence on the body, and the spirit has an enormous influence on the mind. Consequently, spiritual growth may even contribute to the maintenance of physical health as persons age.

Regardless of the influence of spirituality on the mind and body, however, there are reasons to pursue spiritual goals that go way beyond health. In fact, even if some spiritual goals were bad for health, they would still be worth pursuing because, for a people of faith, spiritual development and growth are to be sought after as an end in themselves. Indeed, while life and health here on earth are temporary for all of us, spiritual matters represent things of eternal, immeasurable value that need to eclipse all other priorities.

How does one, then, facilitate spiritual growth in later life? The aging process itself has a way of facilitating spiritual growth that clergy, religious caregivers, even elderly persons, themselves, would be hard-pressed to compete with. Loss, pain, and suffering are the surest goads to spiritual growth. Even in cases when persons become angry at God and turn away from God because of stressful or traumatic life experiences, pastoral caregivers have an opportunity to straightforwardly address issues of faith with them. C. S. Lewis said it well when he wrote, "Pain is God's megaphone to a deaf world." In our work, we've found that persons who become angry at God or turn away from spiritual matters when bad things happen often did not have a truly meaningful relationship with God prior to these events. Seen positively, such traumatic, stressful events may be the catalyst leading to a new or renewed faith relationship for an elderly person. Those who do have a deep and intimate relationship with God usually run toward, not away from, God for comfort when tragedy strikes.

As God is active in our spiritual growth even when we suffer losses and traumatic experiences, what can clergy and religious caregivers do to work with God as partners to facilitate the process of spiritual growth in later life? First, clergy can address the meaning and purpose of pain and loss in their sermons and craft these homilies to meet the emotional needs of physically ill and/or aging persons in their congregations. Even younger adults need to understand the meaning of loss, tragedy, pain, suffering, dependency, and altruism; these topics are applicable to persons of all ages, for pain and love are experienced by young and old alike. Such topics will also make the content of sermons relevant to the daily lives of those in the church.

Second, the focus of church services and church school needs to be directed toward the role of faith in coping with the everyday struggles of life. Indeed, God wants to be involved in our sufferings, failures, and triumphs, in every aspect of our lives, regardless of age. Sermons and lessons that bring God into the daily lives of people as they struggle through their week will foster spiritual growth and bring persons closer to God. Even church potlucks and bazaars might be more directed at meeting the needs of those less fortunate in the congregation or community, again sending the message that fostering spiritual growth and Christ-like lives are the primary mission of the church. Spiritual growth, like any type of growth, is not always pleasant or comfortable.

Third, when counseling older adults who are going through life crises, clergy and religious caregivers should bring God into the situation as part of the solution. Relying on psychological principles and theories to understand and work through problems, while helpful, cannot replace the power of spiritual healing. If elders cannot draw on the strengths and comforts of religious faith or faith in God in working through their problems, then the counselor must thoroughly and carefully explore the person's religious history trying to identify previous negative experiences with religion or current misperceptions about God. These previous experiences may block the person's ability to receive comfort from God in his or her present situation and, once identified, can be reexamined and worked through. Great care should be taken when helping the elderly identify and use spiritual resources to work through their current life situations. A person cannot be forced or bullied into reliance on faith and God. Rather, a flexible, open, and accepting approach on the part of the counselor will meet and establish understanding for the person where he or she currently is. This will set the stage for future progress at the person's own pace along his or her unique spiritual journey that will lead him or her closer to God, closer to his or her fellow human beings, and closer to God's purpose for his or her life.

Fourth, as we repeatedly emphasize throughout this book, elders should be encouraged to use their gifts, talents, and wisdom to serve God by generously giving of their time and talents to meet the needs of others. As one does this, he or she begins to live out the great commandment of loving God and loving neighbor, the hallmark of the Christian life. Finally, elders should be encouraged to develop a routine of regular meditation, Bible study, and worship, both privately and with others. These religious behaviors, when performed sincerely and wholeheartedly, will nourish their souls, foster uplifting bonds of fellowship, and give spiritual strength to love and serve God as they have been called to do.

5

WHAT IS ALZHEIMER'S DISEASE AND WHAT CAN BE DONE?

"You will keep in perfect peace him whose mind is steadfast,
because he trusts in you."
—Isaiah 26:3, NIV

Alzheimer's disease is a progressive brain disease that occurs at increasing frequency with age (5% to 10% of persons over age 65 have the disease, whereas up to 47% of persons age 85 or older have it). Alzheimer's is the fourth-leading cause of death in adults, after heart disease, cancer, and stroke. The onset of the disorder is gradual, insidious, and characterized by declines in: (1) memory (losing objects, repeating stories, missing appointments, learning new information with difficulty), (2) language (difficulty finding the right word when speaking and when naming objects, advancing in the final stages to unintelligible speech and muteness), (3) visuospatial skills (difficulty cooking, setting the table, fixing or manipulating objects in the home), (4) cognition (difficulty handling and manipulating information, performing calculations, making rational judgments), and (5) personality (increased fatigue, indifference, impulsiveness, irritability, self-centeredness, and social withdrawal).

HOW DO YOU MAKE THE DIAGNOSIS?

Alzheimer's disease is a clinical diagnosis. In other words, there are no practical tests that can be done to definitively establish the diagnosis. Brain biopsy and postmortem autopsy are the only ways to make a definite diagnosis of Alzheimer's disease. The diagnosis is made by identifying characteristic pathology in brain cells. Most of the time, however, physicians make a presumptive diagnosis of Alzheimer's disease based on the history from the patient and family, an examination of the patient's memory and other higher brain functions, and certain laboratory tests. In the early stages, it is difficult to distinguish patients with Alzheimer's disease from those with Age-Associated Memory Impairment (the memory impairment associated with normal aging) or cognitive impairment from other causes (multiple strokes, chronic alcoholism, brain tumor, and so forth). In 20% to 25% of cases, the physician's presumptive diagnosis is wrong and some other cause for the patient's symptoms is found at autopsy. It is difficult, then, to establish a diagnosis of Alzheimer's disease after a single evaluation; repeated mental status examinations every six months usually help to clarify the picture.

OTHER CAUSES OF MEMORY LOSS
OR CONFUSION

There are a number of causes of confusion and memory loss other than Alzheimer's disease. These are important to identify because many of the conditions are treatable, unlike Alzheimer's disease. Delirium is a type of confusion that is characterized by a rapid onset, decreased level of alertness and fluctuating level of consciousness; it is usually completely reversible if the underlying cause can be identified and treated. Certain vitamin deficiencies, like B-12 deficiency, can cause symptoms like those of Alzheimer's disease. Other treatable causes include thyroid diseases, syphilis of the brain, and AIDS-dementia.

While Alzheimer's disease is the most common cause of "dementia" (60% to 70%), there are diseases that have similar signs and symptoms. About 15% to 20% of dementias are caused by strokes, and another 5% to 10% are caused by alcohol. Treating blood pressure and taking an aspirin once a day may help prevent further strokes, and cessation of alcohol intake may halt the progression of alcohol-related dementia.

WHAT CAUSES ALZHEIMER'S DISEASE?

We don't know for certain. Hereditary factors play a big role in cases where the disease is genetically transmitted. Other factors play a role in what age the disease begins to show itself, although these are not well understood.

ARE THERE RISK FACTORS FOR
ALZHEIMER'S DISEASE?

Because genetic factors may play a major role in transmission, persons who have relatives with the disease are at greater risk. There may be certain genetic markers for Alzheimer's disease that will enable doctors some day to perform testing to determine a person's chances of developing the condition in the future. These procedures may be able to detect persons with Alzheimer's disease even before they develop symptoms of the disease. These procedures, however, are still in the early stages of development and are not yet available for clinical applications.

WHAT IS THE EXPECTED COURSE
OF ALZHEIMER'S DISEASE?

Alzheimer's disease progresses gradually and slowly through seven fairly distinct clinical stages (Reisberg 1996): (1) *normal* (no symptoms); (2) *Age-Associated Memory Impairment* (normal with symptoms): Person forgets where he or she has placed familiar objects or forgets names of persons that were known previously. There are no other significant problems with memory evaluation. Person has no difficulty at work or in social situations. Person shows appropriate concern for symptoms; (3) *Mild Memory Impairment* (not normal, although not necessarily Alzheimer's disease): Person gets lost when traveling to unfamiliar locations, and his or her work performance declines. Person has difficulty finding words, retains little when reading, and has concentration problems that can be detected on memory testing. Person may deny that there is a problem. This is the

best time to begin estate planning, make out a will, and designate someone as durable power of attorney (for both health and
financial decisions), since persons at this stage still have enough
awareness and insight to direct their resources and future health
care. Estimated duration of this stage is seven years; (4) *mild
Alzheimer's disease:* Person demonstrates decreased knowledge
of current events; some loss of memory for important events in
person's life; and decreased ability to handle finances, travel, or
other complex tasks. Person does not have problems with orien-
tation to time or place, continues to recognize familiar persons
and faces, and does not get lost when traveling to familiar locations. Denial is the major coping behavior. Estimated duration
of this stage is two years; (5) *moderate Alzheimer's disease:* At
this stage, person must have assistance in order to survive. Person is unable to recall things such as major events of his or her
current life, addresses or telephone numbers, names of grandchildren, or name of his or her high school. Person does
remember his or her own name, as well as the names of spouse
and children. Person does not need assistance with toileting or
eating but may need help choosing clothes. Planning for nursing home placement or move to a life-care community is probably wise toward the end of this stage, as many such care facilities
may have long waiting lists. Estimated duration of this stage is
one to two years; (6) *moderately severe Alzheimer's disease:* Person forgets the name of his or her spouse occasionally and is
largely unaware of events in his or her life, although he or she
usually remains oriented to the surroundings and may know the
year and season. At this stage, the person may become incontinent, and his or her sleep cycle may be disturbed (up at night,
sleeps during day). Personality and emotional changes often
occur, like delusional behavior (accuses spouse of cheating,
being an impostor, stealing from him or her), obsessive symptoms, agitation, and sometimes loss of will power (cannot
remember things long enough to carry out actions). This is
usually when caregivers become unable to handle the person
any longer and nursing home placement occurs. Estimated time

WHAT IS ALZHEIMER'S DISEASE

in this stage is two to three years; (7) *severe Alzheimer's disease.* Person's ability to move about independently, walk, speak, communicate, and understand are all lost during this stage. He or she may become incontinent of urine and stool and need assistance in all basic self care activities. Nursing home placement is almost always necessary because of the heavy care demands. Persons generally die approximately two years after onset of this stage, although some may survive for as long as seven years or more.

The time from onset of the disease to death, then, is approximately seven to eleven years, although it can range from only two years to fifteen years or more.

IS THERE ANYTHING THAT CAN BE
DONE ABOUT IT?

We don't know how to prevent the disease or how to cure it. Staying mentally and spiritually healthy as described in chapters 3 and 4 may help to some extent, although even this is uncertain. There are new drugs in development, and one (Aricept®), which may temporarily halt the progression of Alzheimer's disease, is currently being prescribed by doctors. The benefits include possible halting of disease progression or even improvement in some cases. Benefits, however, must be weighed against the cost ($100 or more per month), gastrointestinal side-effects like nausea and diarrhea, and headaches that occur in about 10% of persons. Those with heart arrythmias, seizures, and/or asthma must also be cautious when taking this drug.

We also know a lot about how to manage and care for persons with Alzheimer's disease. This information is invaluable for pastoral caregivers and for caretakers of persons with this disease (see following chapter). Providing support and information to both the person with suspected Alzheimer's disease and his or her caregiver is absolutely crucial to enable them to plan for the future and cope with the distress that Alzheimer's disease brings. Information about the course of Alzheimer's disease and tips about how to deal with legal issues and behavioral problems as the disease progresses can be helpful to pastoral caregivers as well. There are also effective drugs available for controlling the agitation, delusions, and hallucinations seen in about 50% to 70% of persons.

6

HOW CAN CAREGIVERS AND FAMILIES BE HELPED TO COPE WITH THEIR RESPONSIBILITIES?

"The Lord gives strength to his people; the Lord blesses his people with peace."
—Psalm 29:11, NIV

According to the American Association of Retired Persons (1986), more than five million older persons in the United States require some form of assistance to maintain independent living. The vast majority of this assistance comes from elderly spouses (many of whom have health problems themselves) and adult children (many of whom also have work and/or family responsibilities).

Caregivers of older adults with chronic or disabling illnesses frequently experience great emotional and physical stress because of the heavy responsibilities they must shoulder. For caregivers of persons who have dementia or Alzheimer's disease, the burden of care is even greater. In the early stages of Alzheimer's, persons lose their ability to perform usual household chores, which leaves these responsibilities to the caregiver—the bills have to be paid, the meals have to be cooked, the house has to be cleaned, the yard and car need to be maintained. In the later stages of Alzheimer's, demented persons need to be dressed, bathed, and monitored constantly so that they do not wander out of the home or do destructive, dangerous things inside the home (like turning on the stove or gas and forgetting to turn it off). Demented patients may become incontinent of urine and stool, adding further burden on the caregiver.

31

As Alzheimer's progresses, about one-half to three-quarters of patients become delusional, agitated, and may even strike out at caregivers who they may no longer recognize. In the latter stages of Alzheimer's, demented persons cannot be left unattended and require twenty-four-hour supervision. Thus, caregivers can easily become socially isolated because they do not have time to nurture relationships with others. Demented persons often have a reversal of their sleep-wake cycles, being up and active during the night and sleeping during the day. This may cause caregivers sleep deprivation at night and fatigue throughout the day. They may become irritable and impatient with their uncooperative, demented relative and may even physically abuse him or her. It is not at all surprising, then, that depression, anxiety, trouble sleeping, marital conflict, alcohol use, and medical illness are all higher among caregivers (Cantor 1983), and that many end up placing loved ones in nursing homes.

There are many things pastoral caregivers can do to help relieve the burden of those who must care for chronically ill or demented family members. These include providing respite from caregiving responsibilities; companionship and social outlets; practical help; counseling and spiritual support; information about the disease, its course, community resources that may facilitate home care, options for placement; and permission for placement.

RESPITE FROM CAREGIVING RESPONSIBILITIES

Caregivers need to get out of the house on a regular basis. They need to do fun things for themselves at least two afternoons per week. This is absolutely essential to avoid getting burned out. Church members and pastors may take turns spending afternoons with the patient, thus allowing the caregiver some time for him- or herself. Larger churches may sponsor an adult day care that provides structured activities for demented persons for four to six hours per day. Privately run adult day cares may exist in the community, but they are often quite expensive. The church or caring members of the congregation may also help provide the finances to pay for adult day care once a week, although it may be less expensive to simply hire someone to sit for four to six hours per week with the patient at home.

COMPANIONSHIP AND SOCIAL OUTLETS

Simply being a friend and companion to the caregiver can go a long way toward relieving the stress of caregiving and combating the isolation that this task engenders. Call the caregiver on the telephone to check how he or she is doing. Spend time with the caregiver in his or her home. Accompany the caregiver to the doctor's office or other appointments. Take him or her out to a movie or out to dinner. Involve the person in some type of social activity, either in the church or the community. Get to know the person and be a friend to him or her. Members of the church congregation can often fulfill this role as well; however, they must be motivated, know of the need, and realize how important it is to provide such companionship.

PRACTICAL HELP

Offer to drive the caregiver and his or her loved one to the doctor's office or other appointments. Bring a meal on a regular basis. Cut the caregiver's lawn, take care of the yard, clean his or her house, perform repairs on his or her car. The pastor and members of the congregation should do whatever they can to help relieve some of the caregiver's responsibilities.

COUNSELING AND SPIRITUAL SUPPORT

When depression or anxiety impairs the caregiver's functioning, then pastoral counseling becomes necessary. Simply talking about his or her stress to a concerned pastor or trained counselor can help caregivers feel less isolated and alone; it can enable them to vent pent-up feelings and frustrations that otherwise might be internalized. Encourage and show the caregiver how to rely on his or her religious faith and relationship with God to cope with the situation. Research at Johns Hopkins University has shown that caregivers of patients with Alzheimer's disease or terminal cancer adapt much more quickly if they rely on their religious faith (Rabins et al. 1990).

INFORMATION AND EDUCATION

Caregivers need to know what to expect in the days ahead. Pastoral counselors can help caregivers find the necessary resources for information. Having information about the usual course of the illness and about behavioral problems that may occur can help the caregiver achieve some control over his or her situation. On the other hand, providing too much information early on in the disease may only cause unnecessary worry. Pastoral counselors need to be sensitive to how much information the caregiver wants and needs at any particular point in the patient's illness. *The 36-Hour Day* by Mace and Rabins (1981) is an extremely helpful book that frees the caregiver to seek out information at his or her own pace. *The North Carolina Caregiver's Handbook* (NC Division of Aging 1995) provides information about community resources to help care for elders in their homes, to locate housing options and living arrangements for elders, to address legal and financial concerns of elders, and to deal with many other issues that come with aging.

Caregiver support groups exist in most communities and can be located by calling the National Alzheimer's Disease and Related Disorders Association at 1-800-621-0379. Participation of the caregiver in such groups helps to counteract social isolation and provides a forum for sharing experiences. Pastoral counselors can help the caregiver to obtain legal advice about how to draw up a Power of Attorney, make a Will, and complete a Living Will—all are necessary and important tasks that are better completed earlier than later on. Information about placement options (rest home care, nursing home care, special Alzheimer's units) can relieve some of the pressure of caregiving by helping the caregiver develop alternative plans should the burdens of caregiving become too much.

PERMISSION FOR PLACEMENT

Most family members are extraordinarily committed to caring for their loved ones at home. The idea that most families abandon their relatives to nursing homes is a complete myth. Most families go through enormous hardships in order to continue caring for their loved ones at home and to avoid nursing home placement. Nevertheless, there comes a time when placement becomes necessary both for the good of the caregiver and the patient (see chapter 8). Even then, family caregivers often feel extremely guilty about making such decisions. Clergy and physicians are in an ideal position to "give permission" to caregivers to place their loved one in a nursing home and to help them work through the guilt that this decision brings. This guilt, if unaddressed, often interferes with the ability of family members to continue to minister to and spend time with a relative once the person is transferred to the nursing home.

7

HOW CAN COMMUNITY RESOURCES FOR OLDER PERSONS BE LOCATED?

"Love your neighbor as yourself. . . ."
—Leviticus 19:18, NIV

There are many community resources that may help older persons remain living independently in their homes or make the burden of caregiving in the home easier. Older adults, however, often have difficulty navigating through the complex maze of available services and then accessing them. The following is a list of types of community resources available in most middle- to large-size communities (NC Division of Aging 1995):

- *Congregate nutrition programs* provide nutritious meals in group settings, along with opportunities for health, education, social, recreational, and other community services.
- *Employment services programs* include assessment and development of plans to seek employment, testing, counseling about jobs, training, and job placement.
- *Financial counseling programs* provide counseling on money management and budgeting of funds and assists persons in developing plans to overcome large debts or other financial problems.
- *Health promotion and disease prevention programs* involve assessment of health risks, nutrition counseling, exercise and fitness programs, drug education and management, and so forth.
- *Housing counseling programs* assist elders to acquire and maintain housing suitable for their level of functioning.

- *Income tax assistance programs* provide trained volunteers to help elders complete federal and state income tax forms.
- *Information and case assistance programs* help older adults and families obtain services to meet their needs.
- *Legal assistance programs* help in preparation of wills, powers of attorney, and deed changes, and assist elders with locating benefits (Social Security, Medicare, Medicaid).
- *Mental health counseling programs* include consultation, evaluation, and outpatient treatment.
- *Senior centers* are community facilities that provide a wide range of services and activities for elders, including congregate meals, education, and health screening.
- *Volunteer programs* provide opportunities for older adults or younger adults to give of their time and talents to help others.
- *Adult day care programs* provide weekly or daily support for elders in need of supervision and social interaction.
- *Assistive technology equipment, medical equipment, or supplies programs* provide assistive devices (canes, walkers, bathtub equipment) that help elders continue living independently.
- *Care/case management programs* provide assistance from trained social workers or counselors to help elders access and coordinate services to keep them living at home.
- *Emergency response system,* usually in the form of a button on a wristband or a pendant around the neck that an elder may push to summon immediate assistance, alerts the hospital or emergency room if the person needs emergency medical treatment.
- *Financial assistance programs* may provide short-term assistance with food, gas, or medications for elders without sufficient funds to provide for these necessities.
- *Friendly visitor programs* provide volunteers who make weekly visits to homebound elders for socialization and companionship.

- *Home-delivered meals programs* deliver meals to home-bound elders to help them maintain their nutrition.
- *Home health care services* provide skilled help (necessary for the elder to be able to live at home) prescribed by a physician, including registered nurses, aides, occupational therapists, physical therapy, and social workers.
- *Housing rehabilitation programs* provide loans or grants to make minor renovations or repairs to homes, or to make homes more livable for persons with disabilities.
- *Hospice programs* provide a wide range of medical, nursing, social, and psychological services to elders who are terminally ill, with 6 months to live, and their families. Patients may be served at home, in nursing homes, or in the hospital, depending on care needs.
- *In-home aide services,* often designed to keep an elder in the home or to take the burden off the caregiver, provide nurse's aides to help elders with personal care or supervision (can be expensive, for example, $15 per hour).
- *Community long-term care ombudsman* provides advocacy for older adults in nursing homes or rest homes. This person's job is to be sure the elders' rights are protected and to be sure that complaints of residents receive attention.
- *Respite care programs* provide temporary care for older adults so that caregivers can get away from home to shop, run errands, or engage in pleasurable recreational activity.
- *Telephone reassurance programs* provide volunteers who regularly make telephone calls to homebound elders. If any problem is detected, then the volunteer will contact a friend or family member.
- *Transportation services programs,* for a nominal fee, provide transportation (by bus, van, or personal auto) to and from doctor appointments, nutrition sites, or other community activities.

HOW DO PASTORAL COUNSELORS ACCESS
THESE RESOURCES?

Pastoral counselors can call the local *area* agency on aging. These are government-sponsored programs devoted to providing for the needs of the elderly in a particular region. If such an agency cannot be located, then call the county aging services department, county aging services council, cooperative extension services, department of social services, or health department. If still no agency can be located, pastoral counselors can then contact their local library reference desk; the librarians may be able to find the local agency that coordinates such services.

There is also a national service that helps elders and their families find information about community resources and services. Pastoral counselors and caregivers must have the older person's zip code, name, and address available when calling. The number is 1-800-677-1116. Other useful numbers include:

Alliance for Mentally Ill	800-451-9682
American Cancer Society	800-227-2345
Questions About Cancer	800-422-6237
Arthritis Foundation Answer Line	800-283-7800
American Foundation for Blind	800-232-5463
Questions About Diabetes	800-232-3472
Hearing Aid Hot line	800-521-5247
Questions About Incontinence	800-237-4666
Medicare Fraud and Abuse	800-368-5779
National Hospice Organization	800-658-8898
National Lung Line Service	800-222-5864
National Parkinson's Foundation	800-327-4545
Seniors Health Insurance Information	800-443-9354
Social Security Administration	800-772-1213
Social Security/SSI Disability Hot line	800-638-6810

WHO PAYS FOR THESE RESOURCES?

Federal or state programs may pay for some of these services. Some services are provided free or for a nominal fee; other services are private pay and quite expensive.

8

WHAT INFORMATION IS NECESSARY ABOUT NURSING HOMES?

"Choose my instruction instead of silver, knowledge rather than choice gold. . . ."
—Proverbs 8:10, NIV

Nearly 45% of all people reaching the age of 65 will enter a nursing home at some time in their lives (Kemper and Murtaugh 1991); however, only about 5% of older persons are actually living in these settings at any one time. Placing a loved one in a nursing home can be an extremely stressful and painful experience, both for the older adult being placed and for the family caregiver. To make this transition as easy as possible, pastoral counselors can provide information about when nursing home placement is necessary, availability of other living arrangements besides nursing home placement, how to choose a nursing home, and what responsibilities a family has once placement has occurred.

WHEN IS NURSING HOME PLACEMENT NECESSARY?

In most cases, it is better for an older person to be cared for in his or her own home or that of a relative, rather than being placed in a nursing home. Because nursing homes are usually short-staffed and existing staff are underpaid for their work, most nursing homes provide care that is less than optimal. Nevertheless, there does come a time when nursing home placement becomes absolutely necessary, and there are a number of good homes that provide adequate care. If family members are willing and able to involve themselves in the patient's care at the nursing home, then placement often becomes an excellent solution to a very difficult problem.

There are certain signals that nursing home placement is necessary. Can the patient be safely cared for at home? Can he or she be adequately supervised in the home? Caregivers may have outside family or job responsibilities that prevent them from spending twenty-four hours per day with the patient. When a patient reaches the point that he or she can no longer be safely left alone, and no one is available to stay with the patient twenty-four hours per day, then placement becomes necessary for the safety of the patient. Caregiver exhaustion is another impetus for nursing home placement. If the caregiver becomes too physically or emotionally exhausted to continue caring for the patient, then the best thing for everyone concerned is placement. Another reason for placement is if the care demands of the patient are too great or too complex for family caregivers to meet—medical treatments too technical to be handled by home health nurses, agitation or aggression that cannot be controlled in the home, progression of illness so that the condition becomes too severe to be taken care of outside of a hospital setting. Finally, if there are no family members available or willing to care for the patient, and the patient cannot afford to pay for in-home services, then placement in a nursing home becomes the only option.

ALTERNATIVE LIVING ARRANGEMENTS

Depending on the level of care that a person requires, there may be other options besides nursing home placement. These include the following:

Condominiums: An elder may purchase or rent an apartment in a multi-unit complex; health or nursing services are typically not available; common space, like recreational facilities, may be provided for a member fee.

Shared Housing: The elder lives in shared housing with some private living space but shares kitchen, living room, and bathrooms with others; monthly rent usual, but sometimes these programs are supported in part by federal or private funding.

Home Sharing: Home owners and home sharers are brought together into an arrangement such that the home owner collects rent but may reduce or eliminate rent if home sharer agrees to share in household duties.

Rental Apartments: Some communities have large apartment complexes that are reserved for older adults only and include common areas, activities, or meal services.

Subsidized Senior Housing (also known as government-owned or public housing): These units are typically managed by the county housing authority. They often have waiting lists, and eligibility is based on income and risk of homelessness. Qualifying seniors pay a percentage of their income (often 30%) for subsidized housing.

Continuing Care Communities (CCCs, also known as *Life Care Communities,* LCCs): These are located in campus-like or country club settings and offer a wide array of lifetime nursing and health services. These communities are ideal for healthy, financially well-off persons who are looking to retire and not move again. They guarantee that a person's housing, medical, and nursing care will be provided as long as the person lives. They offer different levels of care, all the way from independent living in private cottages or apartments, to assisted living in single- or double-occupancy rooms, to skilled nursing care for persons requiring major assistance and continuous twenty-four-hour supervision. Meals are provided (in a common dining room) along with other services such as housecleaning, linen services, social activities, and transportation. Different CCCs may have exercise facilities, libraries, beauty and barber shops, branch banks, and places of religious worship. These are the optimal living arrangements for older adults because they provide structured social activities and immediate access to nursing and medical care should it be needed.

Continuing Care or Life Care Communities can be expensive, and there is usually a waiting list (sometimes years). A large one-time entrance fee is charged ($80,000–$120,000), plus a monthly fee ($1,500–$2,000 per month). Medical care may be included in this arrangement (at least for Life Care Communities). Contracts vary and none, some, or all of the initial entrance fee may be refunded to the elder or his or her estate if the elder moves or dies. CCCs are not usually regulated by the state department of insurance as a security, and most persons look at their endowment or advance fee as an investment. These communities carefully screen applicants with regard to their physical health and their financial status. These are private for-profit businesses that want to be sure they don't take a loss by admitting the wrong persons. People who are too physically ill or have dementia are not usually allowed in. People who are disabled and not independent are not admitted unless they have a healthy spouse who can care for them. For these reasons, elders must plan far ahead of time (when they are healthy) if they wish to join such a community. CCCs may or may not require that the person purchase long-term care insurance before entry.

For more information about CCCs and LCCs you may write to Senior Living, P.O. Box 1407, Cary, NC 27512, for a reprint of the article "A Lifestyle Option for the Long Term" ($3.00); see also their Web site at http://www.seniorliving.com. Alternatively, you can write to the American Association of Homes and Services for the Aged, 901 E Street NW, Suite 500, Washington, DC 20004-2037 (202-508-9442), and ask for *The Continuing Care Retirement Community: A Guidebook for Consumers* ($6.95); see also their Web site at http://www.aahsa.org.

Independent and Assisted-Living Retirement Communities: Both of these types of retirement communities require a monthly fee ($400–$2,500 per month) and no down payment. Neither, however, offers lifetime care. In independent-living retirement communities, residents have their own apartments and are provided with congregant meals, cleaning services, transportation, and social activities, but residents must be independent and not require any major personal or medical care ($400–$2,500 per month). In assisted-living retirement communities, residents have a room but not an apartment. They also may need to share their room with another person ($1,250–$2,500 per month). Medications are administered, however, and assistance with personal care is provided. To learn more about assisted living, order a free brochure from American Association of Retired Persons (AARP) titled *Assisted Living in the U.S.: A New Paradigm for Older Persons.* Write to AARP at 601 E Street NW, Washington, DC 20059 and ask for publication D15102; see also their Web site at http://www.aarp.org.

The following are types of twenty-four-hour care, institutional settings that vary depending on the amount of nursing care required by the elder.

Adult Foster Care Homes: These provide personal care for a small number of older or disabled adults. Facilities are often not licensed by the state and do not have nursing or medical personnel on premises. Not available in some states.

Rest Homes (also called domiciliary care): These residential facilities provide personal care for persons who are not able to live independently. Meals, transportation, housekeeping, social, and recreational programs are provided. Medications may be administered, especially if there is a licensed practical nurse (LPN) on the premises. Some assistance with personal care is provided. Specialized nursing or medical care, however, is limited. These facilities are licensed by the state. There are generally two types of rest homes, family care homes and homes for the aged.

Family Care Home: This type of rest home provides room, board, personal care, bathing assistance, supervision, and social activities for two to six adults. This type of rest home typically resembles a private home and is located in a residential neighborhood. It resembles an adult foster care home but is licensed and may have licensed personnel on the premises. For a list of these homes, call the nursing home ombudsman in your area.

Home for the Aged: This is a type of rest home that provides the above care for seven or more adults (what most persons think of when the words "rest home" are mentioned).

Nursing Homes (Intermediate Care or ICF): These provide care for older adults who need occasional but not continuous nursing care. They are also called convalescent or extended care homes. Personal care assistance, social activities, and rehabilitation programs are available if needed. A care plan is developed by the nursing staff, physician, patient, and the elder's family. For indigent patients, Medicaid will pay for this level of care. Applications are made through the county department of social services; there are age, income, and asset eligibility criteria.

Nursing Homes (Skilled Care or SNF): These provide around-the-clock nursing care (medical treatments and supervision) for persons who are confined to bed with physical health problems. Nurses carry out orders that are given by the patient's physician. Short-term stays in skilled nursing facilities after hospitalization may be needed for intensive physical and occupational therapy prior to going home to live independently. For indigent patients, Medicaid will pay for this level of care.

Special Care Units: These are usually associated with ICF or SNF, but some may be associated with rest homes. These units provide special care to persons with specific disorders, like Alzheimer's disease. They are more expensive then regular nursing homes because there are more nurses on staff.

HOW DO YOU CHOOSE A NURSING HOME?

There are five basic considerations that go into choosing a nursing home. First, how much does it cost? The average cost of nursing homes in North Carolina is $34,000 per year. Payment for nursing home care comes almost entirely from out-of-pocket costs, unless the person is indigent. If elders cannot pay for private nursing home care, they must settle for a state-sponsored home, paid for by Medicaid at about $20,000–$25,000 per year. There are usually waiting lists, from six to twelve months, for these facilities, and they often do not provide the best care. Medicare pays for only short-term stays, several weeks, after hospital discharge. After that, it pays nothing. If persons can afford the cost—ranging from $30,000 to $60,000 or more per year—of a private nursing home, then there is greater choice and often a shorter waiting list. As soon as the person can no longer afford the costs of a private nursing home, he or she must move to another facility, usually a Medicaid-certified one. Long-term care (LTC) insurance may be helpful in some cases; however, there are many loopholes that insurance companies use to avoid making payments.

The second consideration is reputation in the community. Contact a local social worker or someone who works in the Division of Social Services and ask about what he or she has heard about the home. Ask family members of persons already living in the home if they are satisfied with the care their loved one has received. Be sure a home is Medicaid-certified; this guarantees at least a minimum quality of care and will assure that the government will pay the bills when the elder can't.

The third consideration is location. The closer a nursing home is to the residence of family members, the more likely that family will visit and monitor the care that their loved one receives. The more often a family member visits, spends time with the patient, and gets to know the nursing staff, the better care their loved one is likely to receive.

Fourth, what is the staffing like at the nursing home, especially on holidays and weekends? It is worth making an unannounced visit to the home on one of these days to see what actually happens. It is important that families have an attorney or CPA review the contract for any housing agreement. Be sure to pay attention to what is *not* provided. Pastoral counselors and caregivers wanting more information about how to choose a nursing home can obtain the pamphlet *Guide to Choosing a Nursing Home* by writing to the U.S. Department of Health and Human Services; ask for publication number HCFA-02174, 1993.

FAMILY RESPONSIBILITIES AFTER PLACEMENT

Once nursing home placement has occurred, especially if there has been resistance and conflict over placement, the elder is likely to have difficulty adjusting to his or her new living arrangement. Likewise, the family member who put the elder there will likely be experiencing a lot of guilt. The older adult may be angry, reject family members, and even refuse to see them. Family members, on the other hand, may feel so uneasy about their decision that they avoid visiting or even communicating with their elder loved one. Both situations require intervention, and the clergy or other well-informed members of the church community, are in an ideal position to help out. Clergy and pastoral counselors may decide to visit recently placed older congregants and let them talk about their experiences. Pastoral counselors might also visit the family and help them to vent their feelings of guilt about the situation. Eventually a family meeting involving the patient and family members should be held at the nursing home, and some type of reconciliation should be sought.

A major reason for facilitating reconciliation is to clear the air so that family members will visit and spend time with the elder in the nursing home. Besides assuring that adequate care is received, their visits will also help relieve the loneliness and isolation that the elder may experience in this setting. Note that between 50% and 75% of nursing home residents have dementia, and mentally alert elders suffer the most in these settings because they have relatively few persons with whom they can relate.

Instead, they end up depending heavily on family members to provide them with social interaction and support. Pastoral counselors and church members can play a major role as a surrogate family for these persons by providing monthly visits for counseling, prayer, or receiving Communion. Weekly visits by clergy, members of the congregation, or Sunday school children can do wonders to reduce the elder's isolation and give him or her a sense of being cared for. Also important is to help the elder find purpose and meaning in his or her new life by contributing to the lives of others at the nursing home (Koenig et al. 1997).

Even elders with severe memory impairment and advanced Alzheimer's disease retain the capacity to experience emotion. They sense the caring and kindness, or the lack of it, of those around them. You can minister to severely demented elders by showing concern and care, praying for them, laying hands on them while praying, reading the Bible to them, or singing old hymns to and with them. These are the "sick" persons that Jesus calls us to visit, and, when we do so, we minister to Christ himself (Matt. 25:39-40).

9

HOW DO OLDER PERSONS COPE WITH DISABILITY AND DEPENDENCY?

"He gives strength to the weary and increases the power of the weak.
Even youths grow tired and weary, and young men stumble and fall;
but those who hope in the Lord will renew their strength.
They will soar on wings like eagles; they will run and not grow weary,
they will walk and not be faint."
—Isaiah 40:29-31, NIV

Twenty percent of persons over age 65 require help walking, 10% require help bathing, and 6% require help dressing; 40% of persons over age 85 require help walking, 28% require help bathing, and 17% require help dressing (Tauber 1992). Despite improvements in health care that are extending the length of life, there has not been as much progress in reducing the disabilities that older persons experience (Kane et al. 1990). In fact, during the first half of the next century, the number of severely disabled persons is expected to rise to nearly five times its present level (Kunkel & Applebaum 1992).

Disability, and the dependency associated with it, strongly correlates with depression, alcohol, and drug abuse. Being dependent on others strips a person of his or her identity and self-esteem. Dependency is the thing that elders fear most—nobody wants to be a burden on others. As persons grow older and experience physical health problems, they often have no other choice than to rely on others, sometimes even for their most basic needs. Is it surprising that many would rather die than live for the rest of their lives dependent upon others for their most basic needs? Is it surprising that some elders try to numb their pain with alcohol or drugs?

53

Adjustment to sudden disability and dependency is particularly difficult for a previously independent and self-sufficient elder. This situation is often brought on by a stroke, automobile accident, or a fall accompanied by major injury such as a hip fracture. Even when disability occurs more slowly, as in Parkinson's disease, progressive dementia, arthritis, or other chronic illnesses, getting used to and accepting one's dependency on others can be a great challenge. How much of a challenge this presents, however, depends on an elder's personality, the value he or she places on independence, the fears that he or she has about depending on others, and how willing and understanding the elder's caregivers are.

What can pastoral counselors say, then, to those who are struggling with dependency issues? Pastoral counselors can help them by (1) providing them with adaptive devices, if possible, that will make them more independent and self-sufficient, (2) learning about and trying to understand their situation, (3) listening to and validating their feelings, and (4) gently and sensitively helping them to discover and use the special gifts that God has given them for their particular situation.

MAXIMIZE FUNCTIONAL ABILITIES

By the time pastoral counselors come into contact with disabled elders, most will have done everything possible to reduce their disability by appropriate medical and surgical treatments, by modifying their environments, or by compensating for disability through the use of adaptive devices (canes, walkers, or special instruments to pick up objects off the floor). In some cases, however, older adults may not have received adequate medical care and assessment for correction of their disabilities. Others may be so discouraged about their condition that they have lost the will to make any effort to help themselves. These persons may need referral to a mental health specialist for counseling and possibly a prescription of antidepressant medication to help restore their motivation for self-care. Some disabled elders may simply be unaware of adaptive devices, lack knowledge of where to acquire them, or are unable to afford them. An occupational therapy evaluation, if it has not already been done, will help identify functional deficits that may be corrected. Thus, the pastoral counselor's first step in helping the disabled and dependent person to cope, is to be sure that everything possible medically has been done to correct functional disabilities, that adaptive devices are available to compensate for uncorrectable disabilities, and that the environment in which the person lives is suited for his or her level and type of disability. Once these steps have been taken, the pastoral counselor can help the disabled person learn to accept and cope with the remaining deficits.

LEARN ABOUT THE SITUATION

Before pastoral counselors can minister to the disabled person's emotional needs, they must find out what those needs are and how those needs came about. Pastoral counselors need to get to know the disabled person in order to understand his or her feelings. What was the person like before becoming disabled? What kinds of activities did he or she most enjoy? What gave the person's life meaning and purpose? What did the person respect and value about him- or herself? Did the person ever have negative experiences with family members or close friends who became disabled? What was the person's relationship like with his or her parents upon whom the person depended while growing up? What does disability and dependency mean or signify to the person? Each individual has a unique history that pastoral counselors need to know about before they can truly understand the person's feelings. Once pastoral counselors begin to truly understand the person, the person may open up and allow them to help. It is only through love, friendship, and time that this is accomplished.

LISTEN AND VALIDATE FEELINGS

Once the pastoral counselor has acquired some perspective on the disabled person's situation, he or she is prepared to listen and experience some of the person's pain. *To be effective, the pastoral counselor has to experience the disabled person's pain.* The word *compassion* means "to suffer with." The pastoral counselor cannot truly validate another person's feelings unless he or she has experienced or is experiencing some of the same feelings. People need to feel that others recognize the pain they are feeling. Once they sense that they are really understood, they will allow the pastoral counselor to minister to their isolation and loneliness. Having broken through, the pastoral counselor is in a position to slowly, gradually, lovingly, and wisely lead them out of their prisons of pain and dispair.

HELP THE PERSON REALIZE
HIS OR HER CALLING

Once a trusting relationship has been established, the pastoral counselor has an opportunity to talk with the older person about how God can help in his or her situation. If there is resistance, gently explore with the person his or her negative feelings or resentments toward God. This will help the person work through any unresolved conflicts that may block his or her ability to obtain spiritual support.

As a pastoral counselor, you know that getting someone to respond in faith to God is not something you can do alone. Grace is involved. Many elderly people are ready to make a faith commitment. There is no room, however, for your pushing or prodding them along to speed things up. Be a witness to them in your love, warmth, and commitment; this is all you can do, and, most of the time, it is enough.

Once the person has committed or recommitted his or her life to God, then pastoral counselors can help the person discover God's calling or purpose for his or her particular life circumstances. If the person can recognize and use his or her special

God-given talents or abilities, this will give life meaning and purpose in spite of, and sometimes actually because of, his or her
disabled state (Koenig et al. 1997). The results will be a reviving
of self-esteem, hope for fulfillment in life, and a sense of wholeness that physical and social losses will not be able to take away.
Using his or her special abilities will also make the person less of
a burden on caretakers and will witness to the power of God in
the person's life.

Ministering to chronically ill and disabled persons, even to
those without memory problems, is not easy. Ministering to
those with dementia or Alzheimer's disease, those who cannot
learn new information, is even more challenging. Luckily, pastoral counselors are not alone in their efforts. Chronically ill and
disabled persons are high on God's priority list. If the clergyperson's or pastoral counselor's calling is to minister to the disabled
and dependent (a population that will surpass ten million persons in America within the next thirty to forty years), then he or
she will make the effort and see people helped and emotionally
healed.

HELPING THE PROUD

Older adults are sometimes too proud to accept help. They feel
uneasy when others try to provide for their needs, even when
they truly need help. As noted above, listening and developing
trust are the first steps in bringing these persons to a place where
they can accept help from the pastoral counselor. Some intensely
independent elders, however, will remain resistant. For these
persons, the following strategy often works. Point out to them
that they possess very important gifts that they can choose to use
or not to use. They have the gift of disability that provides others
with the opportunity to serve God by serving them. (This
approach does not work for people who are excessively dependent and use their disability to manipulate others.) For some
independent and proud elders, the above approach can help
them feel like they are doing something for others and are not

just on the receiving end. In fact, this is absolutely true—by allowing others to minister to them, these persons are allowing others to use their gifts to serve God. This is especially true for proud, independent elders because they must make that extra effort to allow others to serve them. Expressing thanks and appreciation for services that others provide is another way disabled persons can use their gift of disability to serve God by ministering to others the philosophy "Love receives what love gives."

10

WHAT CAN OLDER PERSONS DO TO FEEL USEFUL AND NEEDED?

"'For I know the plans I have for you,' declares the Lord, 'plans to prosper you and not to harm you, plans to give you hope and a future.'"
—Jeremiah 29:11, NIV

As persons grow older, they begin to lose the ability to perform activities and roles that gave their lives meaning when they were younger. Their children grow up and leave home. Persons retire or are retired from their work. A spouse is lost through death. Physical disability prevents involvement in prior hobbies and interests. Younger persons replace them in their positions of authority in the workplace and in the community. Because of these types of losses, many older persons begin to question their value in society and begin to wonder if anyone really needs them. From a secular perspective, the answer to this question may be a realistic no. Society sends many messages to older persons, telling them that they should get out of the way and make room for younger people.

These messages will become louder and louder as younger persons are asked to pay higher and higher taxes to support medical care and living costs for seventy million aging baby boomers. Many older persons, however, do not want to get out of the way and make room for younger persons. They don't want to be told to go off somewhere and not be a bother to anyone. Many elders still want to feel needed by others, want to contribute to society, and are not content to withdraw from life and wait for death.

How can older persons feel useful and needed? What can they do that will make society, largely under control by younger persons, need them or value their experiences? Not a whole lot. But that's all right, because whether or not younger persons feel that older adults have a contribution to make to society is largely irrelevant. There are plenty of things for elders to do right now and in the days ahead. Older adults can choose to take on new roles and tasks that are different from their old ones yet are perhaps even more important for the future of our society.

How is this possible? Elderly people can—if they will—participate in God's love for the world by helping to meet, to the degree they are able, the needs of others, particularly the needs of other elders. The needs of many elders are already not being met in some parts of the United States, and this will continue and worsen as the population of older adults in this country doubles over the next twenty years. There will be increasingly widespread unmet emotional and physical needs among the elderly (Koenig et al. 1994; Callahan 1996). Here is where the church members and pastoral counselors come in and where elderly congregants have an opportunity to engage in the greatest ministry of their lives—*ministry to each other.*

We return again to the need to discover our unique, God-given gifts and talents for the time, age, and situations we are in. There is potential in every situation for people of faith to serve God and bring about a greater good (Romans 8:28). The majority of the elderly still possess talents or abilities that enable them to meaningfully contribute to the work of God's kingdom. Some of these gifts and talents are obvious, others are less obvious and have to be searched for. Those elders who have a faith relationship with God and who have committed themselves to serving God's people will not struggle to feel useful or needed. Those not choosing to use their gifts and talents to help others may experience feelings of purposelessness and uselessness. Pastorally these negative emotional feelings may actually serve a purpose in motivating persons into a new way of thinking, believing, and behaving.

While it may be relatively easy to see how a retired carpenter, electrician, or nurse might use his or her talents to benefit others, what about those with less obvious gifts and abilities? What about the dependent chronically ill or disabled older person who perceives that he or she does not have any abilities or talents that would be needed? Pastoral counselors can help that person to reframe his or her situation.

Take as an extreme example the case of a bed-bound elderly woman who has experienced a stroke that has left her completely disabled. She requires nurses to turn her every two hours to avoid bedsores, to clean up her urine and stool, and even to feed her. This woman might be led to see that, in her situation, serving God's people—and thus God—is as simple as her ability to smile and show appreciation to her caregivers each time they provide care. Perhaps it is her ability to make every possible effort to turn herself and participate in her own care so that the burden on others is reduced. Such a pleasant and considerate attitude in this woman's situation is likely to have a real impact on her caretakers in many different ways. It may brighten an otherwise dreary day for an overworked nurse, who may consequently provide better care to many other patients during his or her shift because he or she feels a little more appreciated. If the disabled woman's motivation is to serve God by serving others, then her actions will result in a sense of meaning and usefulness to her life.

Now that they are no longer raising children or actively employed in the work force, many older adults have the precious gift of time. Volunteering that time to take a meal to someone in need, offering a ride to church to someone without transportation, and sitting for a couple of hours with a person with Alzheimer's disease are just a few examples of how this gift can be used. In *Gospel for the Mature Years* (Koenig et al. 1997), many illustrations are given of older persons using their gifts and talents to serve God.

The church can facilitate this process by assigning a pastoral staff person or a dependable lay leader to keep track, by making lists, of the needs of older persons in the congregation. A second list should be drawn up that details the talents or abilities of each of the elders. Thus, pastoral counselors should encourage every older person to identify gifts or talents that could be used to serve others, as well as indicate their own needs. These talents and needs should then be brought together by a matchmaking process. The ideal result is that every person both has his or her needs met and meets the needs of someone else in the congregation. All are serving God. All are feeling that their lives have purpose and meaning because they are needed by their peers.

Some older adults who feel useless, however, may be experiencing a depressive disorder that causes feelings of worthlessness or uselessness. If an underlying depressive disorder is present, the elder may not be able to identify his or her gifts or use them to serve others. In that case, however, there will usually be other symptoms of depression (see chapter 13). If the elder is depressed, then treatment becomes a first priority.

HOW GOD USES PEOPLE

How can the life of someone who is severely dependent, demented, or even unconscious have meaning or purpose? We are an action-oriented society that does not value being the recipient of care, nor do we really value those who need such care or ministry. Demented or uncommunicative persons may passively participate in God's love for the world by providing others with an opportunity to provide love and care for them. Take, for instance, an elderly grandparent who is unable to communicate because of advanced Parkinson's disease. He or she may receive joy from watching grandchildren become less self-centered and more focused on others as their parents take them to visit their elderly grandparent in the nursing home. Alternatively, a severely disabled elderly person may see emotional and spiritual maturation in a relative who must put his or her own needs second to the disabled person's needs. The pastoral role is to help both caregivers and elders recognize the mutuality of meaning, purpose, and joy in the reciprocity of caring and being cared for. Pastors and religious caregivers can educate elders and their families about the important roles that human beings, regardless of physical or mental state, can play in God's love for the world.

11

HOW CAN OLDER PERSONS WHO FEEL LONELY AND ISOLATED BE HELPED?

"God sets the lonely in families. . . ."
—Psalm 68:6, NIV

More than 20% of men over age 75 live alone compared to almost 55% of women. Almost 50% of women over age of 65 are widows (Saluter 1992). Loneliness is a common problem among older persons, particularly among those who have recently lost a spouse or other close friend. Because of health and financial problems, some older adults may be forced to move out of their homes and communities into living situations where they do not know their neighbors. If such elders are not extroverts by nature, they may not readily reach out to others to form relationships. Physical illness itself is extremely isolating for many older adults. Health problems restrict activity that is necessary to generate and maintain social relationships. Medical illness saps energy and reduces the desire for social participation.

No one really understands what it is like to be sick except the sick person. Despite this, chronically ill persons often have a deep urge within them to try to bridge this isolation by talking to others about their health. Most people, however, don't like to listen to these health complaints and frequently refer to people who discuss them as hypochondriacs. For that reason, despite a need to talk about the tremendous toll that their medical conditions have taken on their lives, elderly persons learn to keep health problems to themselves, further deepening their sense of isolation.

One simple way to help elders who appear lonely and isolated is for the pastoral counselor to visit them at home. Another option is to call them on the telephone. More than 80% of non-institutionalized persons over the age of 85 can still use the telephone without assistance (Tauber 1992). Even a brief telephone call from their pastor or other members of the congregation will reassure them that they are still part of a church community. Lack of time, which is a real concern for all of us in the helping professions, cannot discourage clergy from at least occasionally making these calls themselves. Pastors need to call for other members of the congregation to likewise reach out to those in need of fellowship. There are numerous biblical passages that can be the center of such pastoral messages (Matt. 25:31-46; Luke 10:30-37; 1 John 3:11-24, 4:7-21).

Clergy may also encourage their pastoral staff to acquire volunteers from the congregation to form a visitors team. Members of this team take turns visiting shut-ins or other elderly persons who would otherwise receive little contact. Elders who resist such visits at first are often those who need them most; gentle and loving persistence will usually break through the resistance. The positive effects of such visits have been scientifically demonstrated. A study showed that isolated elderly people who received regular social visits in their homes for six months were more likely to be living independently at the end of the six months than were elders who did not receive these visits (Mulligan and Bennett 1977).

In counseling elders who complain of feelings of loneliness, it is important to listen to them and validate their feelings. Let them talk about their health problems, the death of loved ones, the changes in their lives, or whatever else they need to vent about; there is no need for the pastoral counselor to talk, since these persons need someone to listen to them more than they need someone to give them advice. After several meetings with such persons, it may be necessary to gently and patiently encourage them to visit or telephone other persons in the congregation who are lonely. The best solution to loneliness and isolation is for the older adult him- or herself to try to be a friend to others. The same principle works over and over again; try to relieve someone else's loneliness and you will find that yours may vanish as well. While it may be difficult for these persons to reach out to others to relieve their own loneliness (because of their vulnerability to rejection), they may be willing to do something kind for others.

Some elders, however, become so focused on their own needs that they cannot move beyond themselves to bring comfort to others; instead, they will insist that only the pastor or religious caregiver can relieve their loneliness. Although hard-line tactics should not be taken until many contacts with the person have been made and a solid pastoral relationship established, sometimes a firm stand needs to be taken with persons who refuse to comfort those whom you suggest to them. You may need to make your visits conditional on their doing their part by calling others.

LONELINESS AND GOD

Developing and nurturing a relationship with God is the way many persons cope with loneliness. When they lie in bed awake at night, they can always talk to God. When they are in pain, afraid, or otherwise in distress, they can talk to God about their feelings. Someone once said that humans were created with a hole in their hearts that only God can fill. As long as we try to fill that hole with other things, there will be an emptiness; sometimes that emptiness is interpreted as loneliness. Putting God where God rightfully belongs in our lives may help to bring peace and wholeness to our hearts.

In addition to this deep, abiding need that each of us has for God, the Creator has seen fit to make humans with social needs. The Scriptures are clear that God wants us to fill those needs through fellowship with others (Heb. 10:24-25). For this reason, persons who are lonely and healthy enough should be encouraged to involve themselves in the religious community. If transportation is an issue, then members of the congregation should be recruited to pick up elders on Sunday mornings and whenever there are church services or social functions that they are willing to attend. In this way, elders will have contact with others, increasing the likelihood that social relationships that may combat loneliness will develop. Again, pastors should give sermons that are strong and clear in their emphasis on the need for God's people to reach out and invest in each other's lives, to inspire members of the congregation to meet each other's social needs, including those of older members.

Reading the Bible and other inspirational literature is a way that older persons can occupy their minds so that their thoughts do not become fixated on longings for deceased loved ones or for the glorious days of the long gone past. God speaks to us in Scripture, and those consoling words and many promises have power to dispel loneliness.

LEGAL ASPECTS OF TRANSPORTING ELDERS

One way to reduce the loneliness and isolation of older persons, as noted above, is to provide transportation for them to Sunday church services or to church social functions. What are the legal liabilities of doing so? Can the church be sued? Can the individual volunteering his or her time to transport an elder be sued? Yes, either or both can be sued. How can churches reduce this liability? If a member of the congregation volunteers to occasionally transport older adults to church, then the person should contact his or her automobile insurance company and find out what needs to be done in order to extend liability coverage to include "incidental use" for transporting elders. Often, there is little or no extra premium for this addition. Second, the pastor or staff should talk with the church's liability insurance company and find out what is necessary to extend liability coverage to include members volunteering their time to transport elders to church. Most church policies are so broad that they may already cover this, but this needs to be clarified and probably put in writing. If the church owns a bus that goes out and transports elders, then the pastor should be sure the vehicle coverage includes liability for transporting elders. If a church relies on paid help to drive a bus, then liability increases dramatically compared with the use of volunteers. If church services are being held in a place that is rented (like a shopping center or other vacant building that is not owned by the church), then the liability coverage may not be as good as if the congregation owned the building (renter's insurance vs. home owners insurance) and additional coverage may be necessary.

SMALL GROUP MINISTRY

As noted before, pastors and pastoral staff cannot do all the ministry, counseling, emotional support, visitations, and fulfillment of other needs that older or chronically ill persons have. For this reason, we have suggested that small groups of persons, each consisting of about ten older and younger persons, be created within the church (Koenig et al. 1997). These small groups meet in the homes of persons in the congregation who volunteer to be group leaders (as approved by the pastor). These small groups meet once a week and have a number of functions, including discussing the sermon, studying the Bible, praying, having fellowship, and eating together. People in the congregation choose which home group they wish to be a part of and are responsible for attending the group. The pastor emphasizes the importance of these groups and encourages participation.

These small groups mimic the family and serve two major functions. First, they are places where people in the congregation can use their gifts and talents to serve the needs of others in their home group. Second, these groups serve an important function in reducing the isolation and loneliness of their members. In this way, ministry to older adults is spread throughout the church body.

12

HOW CAN FAITH HELP OLDER PERSONS COPE WITH CHRONIC ILLNESS?

"My flesh and my heart may fail, but God is the strength of my heart and my portion forever."
—Psalm 73:26, NIV

The ten most common chronic medical conditions among non-institutionalized persons age 65 or over in the United States are arthritis (49%), high blood pressure (39%), hearing impairment (31%), deformity or orthopedic impairment (17%), cataract (15%), heart disease (14%), visual impairment (10%), diabetes (9%), stroke (6%), and chronic bronchitis (6%) (Havlik et al. 1987). In a recent study at Duke Hospital of eighty-seven elderly patients who had multiple chronic medical illnesses and were in great distress over their conditions, those who scored highest on intrinsic religiosity (or personal faith in God) recovered significantly faster from emotional distress than did persons with lower intrinsic religiosity (Koenig et al. 1998). In fact, having strong religious faith had an even greater effect on emotional healing than did changing physical health and functioning. These results provide solid scientific evidence that intrinsically motivated faith helps persons to cope with chronic physical health problems.

How, then, can clergy and religious caregivers facilitate this process? We have asked elderly patients themselves how they have used their religious faith to help them better cope. Their responses vary tremendously. Perhaps the most common response is "by placing trust and faith in God." Many elders said that they simply turned their situations over to God and let God take care of them. They were then able to stop worrying and stop trying to work the situations out by themselves. It is the preoccupation with and ruminating over a situation the person cannot change that generates negative emotions. These persons were able to stop worrying about their situations by releasing them to God (after doing what they could to solve the problems). Of course, many of these elders tried to take the problem back from God and struggled with it again, but they learned not to do this. Other elderly patients said they coped through prayer. Praying to God somehow brought them comfort. Even though they did not have any control over their situations, they believed that God did, and God would respond to their prayers and take care of things. This brought consolation and relief from worry or depression.

Reading the Bible or other inspirational literature was another way that older patients frequently coped. Again, many could not describe why this made them feel better, but it did. Some said that singing religious hymns lifted their spirits. Others remarked how visits and prayers from clergy and church friends were helpful in enabling them to cope with health problems. Knowing that everyone had prayed for them during the church service often brought great comfort. Attending church themselves was very important to many elderly patients, who often went to extraordinary lengths to get to church despite functional limitations.

These responses give clues about how clergy and religious caregivers can help persons use their faith to help them to cope with chronic illness. First, elders need to have a relationship with God and must believe that God has their best interests at heart. If existence here on earth is not simply a random or chance event of nature, then there must be some purpose and greater design for our continued presence here—even when we are sick and disabled. If God is responsible for our being here, not ourselves or random chance, then we should realize that God must be present in the life of a sick, elderly, or disabled person. Helping elders to realize that God is steadfastly present, has their best interests at heart, and has a purpose for their lives will give them a sense that they are not alone in their struggle, nor are they in the hands of aimless fate. Having done everything they can to help solve their problems, they must learn to stop struggling and let God do the rest. If elders cannot do this, then they may need help working through trust issues. Explore with them in an open and accepting manner their doubts and difficulties believing or trusting in God. Just talking about it often helps them resolve their uncertainties.

Second, our elderly patients prayed a lot. They talked with God as if God were right there with them in the room. Some persons said that family members often didn't really understand them and, instead, had their own interests at stake. God, on the other hand, really knew them and understood everything that they were going through. Again, this made elders feel less alone. Thus, encouraging patients to talk with God about their fears and deepest concerns can help to counteract the isolation that accompanies chronic illness. Praying with patients and laying on of hands are also important because these actions reaffirm belief in God and communicate to the elder that they are part of a caring Christian community. Particularly effective are prayer groups or prayer chains that commit to praying for those in need; if the elder knows that he or she is being prayed for by others in the church family, this will comfort and bring hope to the elder.

Third, our patients said that reading the Bible and other inspirational literature brought comfort. Chronically ill elders might be given passages from the Bible that are particularly applicable to their situation and encouraged to think about and meditate on these passages. Biblical role models exist for almost every situation, especially for persons facing illness or tragedy in their lives—for example, Job, David, Jeremiah, Paul. Discuss biblical passages with older adults, find out what these passages say to them, and listen as they reflect on the biblical truths. Remember that your opinions and advice are less important than your willingness to listen and allow elders to think aloud as they work through their own thoughts and feelings.

Fourth, depending on the elder's faith tradition, religious rituals may be comforting and convey a sense of God's presence. Examples of such rituals include Holy Communion, confession, or other ritualistic blessings performed by the pastor. Providing elders with the opportunity to attend church and participate in these rituals may be quite important in helping them cope with their illnesses. Receiving Communion, for many elders, reminds them of how Christ suffered and died for them, reaffirming God's deep love and commitment. Whether confession is ritualized as in the Roman Catholic tradition, or whether it is spontaneous and personal as in the Protestant tradition, it is important that chronically ill elders be given an opportunity to confess their sins, which may be preventing them from turning to God in their present difficulties.

Thus, there are many ways that clergy and religious caregivers can help older adults use their religious beliefs to cope with chronic illness. Encourage them to use their faith; provide them with religious materials and circumstances that may facilitate this; and allow them to talk about and work through distrust of God, negative experiences with religion, or guilt over past sins. All of these actions can help the elder access effective spiritual resources (Weaver, Koenig, and Roe 1998).

13

HOW CAN OLDER PERSONS WHO ARE DEPRESSED, GRIEVING, OR SUICIDAL BE HELPED?

"May the God of hope fill you with all joy and peace as you trust in him,
so that you may overflow with hope by the power of the Holy Spirit."
—Romans 15:13, NIV

Depression is the most common treatable psychiatric illness in old age. It affects up to 15% of persons age 65 or older in the United States and increases to nearly 25% of those in nursing homes (National Institutes of Health 1991). Only about 10% of elders with emotional distress receive any treatment from mental health professionals. Many seek out clergy for help. Surveys indicate that depression is at the top of the list among problems brought to pastors, and pastors recognize a need for additional training in depression awareness and treatment (Weaver 1995). Researchers have discovered that clergy are most often sought for counseling in crisis situations associated with grief or depressive reactions such as: personal illness or injury, death of a spouse, death of a close family member, divorce or marital separation, change in health of a family member, and death of a close friend (Weaver 1993). A Gallup survey found that seniors are more willing to turn to clergy than either medical doctors or mental health specialists for help when a friend is contemplating suicide (Gallup 1992).

WHAT IS DEPRESSION?

The feelings of depression are some of the worst pains imaginable. They emanate deep from within the chest and seem to go on and on without relief. The pain causes a person to sink into a deep blackness out of which there appears no escape, no hope, no future. Those who have this illness are truly imprisoned, oppressed by their own emotions. Christ said that he had been sent "to heal the brokenhearted, to preach deliverance to the captives . . . to set at liberty them that are bruised " (Luke 4:18 of Jesus quoting Isaiah 61:1 KJV). Our calling, as pastoral care-givers, is a similar one.

Depression is a treatable emotional disorder, not a normal consequence of aging. Depression is not like the minor mood fluctuations that all of us may have during the course of a day or week. Instead, depression is an enduring disturbance in mood that interferes with a person's ability function in his or her work or social relationships. Depression is far from a benign condition and has a lifetime mortality rate of 15%. Major depressive disorder, the more severe variety of depression, is defined by certain criteria: two weeks or more of feeling sad, down in the dumps, or disinterested in things plus at least four of the following eight symptoms (during the two weeks): (1) loss of weight and decreased appetite or increased appetite and weight gain; (2) difficulty sleeping or sleeping too much; (3) loss of energy, fatigue; (4) decreased concentration; (5) moving about more slowly or excessive restlessness and agitation; (6) loss of sexual interest; (7) feelings of worthlessness or feeling like a burden; and (8) feeling the desire to die. The following questions may be helpful in determining whether or not someone is depressed:

- Does the person feel sad or irritable?
- Has the person lost interest in the things that once gave him or her pleasure (job, hobbies, friends, sex)?
- Has the person's appetite or weight changed?
- Has the person's sleep pattern changed; is the person sleeping too much or not enough?
- Does the person feel tired all the time or have no energy?
- Does the person feel hopeless, worthless, or like he or she is a burden on others?

- Does the person have trouble concentrating, remembering things, or making decisions?
- Have the person's friends noticed that he or she has been more restless than usual or that his or her activity has decreased?
- Does the person often think about death or wanting to die? Has the person thought about wanting to commit suicide? (An answer of yes to either of these counts as yes to the entire question.)

If a person answers "yes" to five or more of the above questions, then he or she should be referred to a physician for treatment.

Depression is thought to be caused by an imbalance of chemicals in the brain, especially serotonin. A person may be vulnerable to depression either because of hereditary factors or because of traumatic experiences in childhood. Severe brief stress or long-term moderate to severe stress can lead to depression in a susceptible person; the more vulnerable the person is to depression, because of inherited factors or because of childhood trauma, the less stress is necessary to bring on depression. Every person, regardless of vulnerability factors, given sufficient stress for a long enough period, is capable of becoming depressed.

WHAT TREATMENTS ARE AVAILABLE FOR DEPRESSION?

Depression can be improved in almost all cases by one of three types of treatment: psychotherapy, antidepressant medication, and electroshock therapy. The milder forms of depression respond very well to psychotherapy, whereas the more severe forms require medication or electroshock therapy.

The four most common types of psychotherapy used to treat depression in older adults are cognitive-behavioral therapy (CBT), interpersonal therapy (IPT), reminiscent therapy (RT), and supportive therapy (ST). In CBT, there is an attempt to change depression-producing beliefs and attitudes to healthier,

more realistic ones; behaviors that produce pleasure and fulfillment are also encouraged. Many depressed older adults define
their life situation with global statements like "everything is
hopeless," "nothing is working out," "I'm totally stupid," "I'm
old and useless," or "I can't do anything right." Depressed individuals tend to conclude the worst, dwell on negative details, and
devalue the positive. CBT seeks to stop or modify these pes-
simistic automatic thoughts, which people use to define themselves, their environment, and their future. If these beliefs go
unrecognized and unchallenged, such distortions in thinking will
result in continued depression. It is critical that this sort of dis-
torted thinking is interrupted. Usually treatment involves self-
monitoring of thoughts and activities, often in the form of keeping a daily log. Pastors working with depressed individuals will
find the books *Feeling Good, The New Mood Therapy* (Burns
1980) and *You Can Beat Depression* (Preston 1996) to be practical guides with step-by-step approaches on how to use CBT
effectively.

IPT is a type of psychodynamic therapy that looks at a person's past and present relationships and tries to help the person
work through conflicts in them. RT is a treatment in which the
person is encouraged to perform a life review and come to terms
with things in his or her past that are contributing to current difficulties. ST is the most effective type of therapy when a person
has experienced a recent severe stress, trauma, or loss, and needs
support from others to cope with the experience. ST is often the
therapy that older adults suffering from social or physical health
losses need the most. More severe depressions, especially those
associated with suicidal thoughts, weight loss, and other biological symptoms of depression, require the use of antidepressant
medication in conjunction with psychotherapy.

Antidepressants are often rapidly effective in the treatment of
depression. These drugs act by restoring the level of brain chemicals, such as serotonin and norepinephrine, that become deplet-
ed when persons become depressed. Significant improvement
may occur in sleep and mood during the first week of treatment;

maximum effect, however, is not usually achieved until six to eight weeks of treatment. There are many different types of anti-depressants. The type of antidepressant that is best for a particular individual depends on drug side effects, the type of symptoms the person is having, and the particular physiological makeup of the person. Sometimes, several antidepressants may need to be tried before the right one is found. Persons do not become addicted to antidepressants like they do to minor tranquilizers (such as Valium®), sleeping pills, or narcotics for pain. If persons stop using an antidepressant suddenly, however, they may experience a mild withdrawal reaction, a flu-like syndrome.

Persons who do not respond to antidepressants or who have life-threatening symptoms of depression (serious suicidal impulses or weight loss threatening survival) need immediate treatment. Electroshock therapy, ECT, is remarkably effective and safe in treating severe depressions in older adults, particularly those with paranoia or delusions. ECT may actually have fewer side effects than antidepressant medication, when used by frail, medically-ill older patients. New methods of administering ECT have completely revolutionized this form of treatment, making it both safer and more effective.

WHAT CAN BE DONE TO HELP ELDERS WITH DEPRESSION?

For elders with more severe forms of depression, the best thing pastoral counselors can do is encourage them to see a physician who can provide them with necessary treatment. Remember that 15% of persons with depression end their lives by suicide, so this is a serious emotional disorder that requires specialized treatment.

Mild forms of depression, particularly those associated with loss of loved ones or with physical health problems, are often helped by having someone to talk to, someone who will listen to the elder and try to understand what he or she is going through. These depressions are often closely related to, if not synonymous with, grief. Successful grieving requires that a person talk about and work through his or her loss. Having another person to share painful feelings with, who wants to understand the feelings and is willing to help carry their burden, can greatly facilitate the grieving process. Nevertheless, working through grief always requires time, and it may take longer for older adults because they are often grieving over several losses at once (for example, loss of independence, loss of loved ones, loss of finances or possessions, and loss of role or position). Major losses usually take between three and six months to work through. For a more detailed description of different types of depression and grief and cases that illustrate their presentation and management, see *Counseling Troubled Older Adults* (Koenig and Weaver 1997). For a sensitively written text on the dynamics of grief among older persons, see *Losses in Later Life: A New Way of Walking with God* (Sullender 1985). This book is a masterpiece that will be helpful to pastors and laypersons.

DEPRESSION AND GOD

Research has shown that psychotherapy, which uses religious beliefs and activities as part of the therapy, is more rapidly effective in relieving depression in religious persons than is traditional, secular psychotherapy (Propst et al. 1992). Furthermore, medically ill older persons who are depressed and score high on intrinsic religiosity recover more quickly from depression whether they receive any specific treatment for their depression or not (Koenig et al. 1998). Thus, clergy and religious caregivers have powerful tools at their disposal to help combat depression and hopelessness: faith in God, prayer, Scripture, and worship. An older person's religious faith may be one of the most effective ways of combating depression and a caregiver's failure to use religious faith as a resource does the elder a grave disservice.

Be aware, however, that depression can make it much harder for elders to access spiritual resources. Depressed persons may cry out repeatedly to God, who appears not to be responding. They may begin to feel deserted by God and angry about their pain. Depressed persons may also find it very difficult to read the Bible, pray, or even attend church services. Pastoral counselors must be patient with them. Encourage them to do what they can, even if it is only to momentarily cry out to God for help. Patience and caution are necessary because depressed persons are already vulnerable to feeling guilty because of the depressive disorder itself. Every effort should be made to avoid arousing guilt over depressed persons' inability to engage in religious practices.

WHEN SHOULD PASTORAL COUNSELORS REFER ELDERS TO MENTAL HEALTH SPECIALISTS?

Even grief can deepen into a major depressive disorder that will require more help than you are able to give. The following are signals that should alert pastoral counselors to the need for a referral: Persistent sadness and inability to experience pleasure that shows no signs of improvement after several weeks of counseling; more than 5 lbs. of weight loss or more than 10 lbs. of weight gain; severe problems with sleep (either not sleeping or sleeping too much); severe fatigue or slowing of movements; marked irritability, agitation, or restlessness; any strange ideas or paranoia (delusions); any suicidal thoughts or longing to die; and if you become uncomfortable for any reason when counseling the person.

WHAT DO PASTORAL COUNSELORS NEED TO KNOW ABOUT SUICIDE?

Being alert to the signs and symptoms of impending suicide is of utmost importance, whether or not the elder is also seeing a mental health specialist. In fact, studies have shown that nearly 75% of suicides occur within one month of seeing a doctor. The older adult is even more likely to have contact with his or her pastor or pastoral counselor prior to attempting suicide (Weaver et al. 1996; Weaver and Koenig 1996). Persons at highest risk for suicide have the following characteristics: prior history of suicide attempts; depression and alcohol abuse; restless, agitated, or anxious type of depression; chronic disabling or painful medical condition; memory problems or confusion; hopelessness about situation and seeing no way out; and few family, friends, or supportive relationships. Older white males, especially if widowed or divorced, are particularly at risk for suicide.

Always ask a person with depression about suicidal thoughts, no matter how mild the case may appear. Studies have shown that caregivers will not give the person an idea or increase the likelihood of suicide by asking about it. It is best to approach the topic slowly and gently. First ask if the person has ever wondered if life was worth living like this, or wondered whether it might be better if he or she simply died. Second, if the response is yes, then ask if the person has ever thought about hastening things along. Third, if the person has thought about this, then ask whether the he or she has thought about doing that recently. Fourth, if so, then ask if the person has thought about how he or she might do it. Lastly, if the person has a plan, then ask when he or she is planning to do it. Don't try to discourage the person, simply listen, try to understand his or her pain, and get information.

Any positive responses to the third question (or fourth or fifth questions) require that you take action to ensure the person's safety for the moment and then get him or her to see a mental health specialist. If the elder is unwilling to see a mental health specialist and your level of concern is great enough, then contact family members and urge them to fill out commitment papers at the magistrate's office. These papers will direct the sheriff to bring the person in for psychiatric evaluation against his or her will. If no family is available, then the pastor or pastoral counselor must fill out the commitment papers. If the situation is more urgent, simply call 911 or the sheriff's office.

14

HOW CAN OLDER PERSONS WHO ARE ANXIOUS AND FEARFUL BE HELPED?

"God is our refuge and strength, an ever present help in trouble. Therefore we will not fear. . . ."
—Psalm 46:1-2, NIV

There are many realistic things that older persons worry about. They worry about their safety and vulnerability to assault and robbery. They worry about declining finances. They worry about having to sell their homes and move into nursing homes. They worry about their health and the health of loved ones. They worry about becoming disabled and dependent on others. They worry about being left all alone. Death is often the least of their worries.

Despite the many things older adults have to worry about, only about 6% of persons over age 65 have anxiety disorders that require psychiatric treatment. The most common types of anxiety disorder are panic disorder (two to five minutes of severe anxiety associated with racing heart and breathlessness) and generalized anxiety disorder (feeling anxious all the time). For these persons, medical treatments are very effective in relieving their symptoms. For immediate relief of panic symptoms, benzodiazepines (such as lorazepam or alprazolam) are the drugs of choice. Nevertheless, these medications can be habit-forming and have numerous side effects in the elderly, such as interfering with memory, altering balance, and causing oversedation. The use of antidepressants to relieve anxiety symptoms is much safer, not habit-forming, and equally effective; however, antidepressants may take longer to work, as long as four to six weeks. Combination treatment with both a benzodiazepine and an antidepressant is usually prescribed for the first couple weeks of therapy; once the antidepressant begins to take effect, the benzodiazepine can be gradually withdrawn. Given the widespread use of medications to treat emotional problems, it is wise to have a basic text on medications in the church library. *Clinical Psychopharmacology Made Ridiculously Simple* (Preston and Johnson 1995) is a readable, well-organized book. When pastors have been asked to give reasons that they do not refer more individuals to mental health professionals, fear of overmedication of parishioners was one reason.

Many older adults, however, have less severe anxiety and fears that interfere with their lives but do not require drug therapy. For these fears and worries, cognitive-behavioral therapy (CBT) is very effective. CBT may involve providing new information, teaching problem-solving strategies, correcting skill deficits, modifying ineffective communication patterns, and changing the physical environment in which problems arise. As noted before, however, CBT's primary goal is to change the way older persons think about themselves and about the events that are occurring around them. CBT includes discouraging catastrophic thinking or worry about the disasters that might happen. This re-educative therapy trains elders to monitor their thoughts and challenge those that are anxiety-provoking.

For example, the thought, "If I get sick and lose my independence, it will be the worst thing in the world. I won't be able to stand it!" might be changed to, "If I get sick and lose my independence, which may not ever happen, it will be difficult for me, but I'll be able to handle it with God's help." The behavioral part of CBT involves training persons to relax and breathe properly so that they can do something on their own to reduce their anxiety. While these are specialized psychotherapeutic techniques, they are learned relatively easily. There are even popular books that describe how people can learn these techniques on their own. *Telling Yourself the Truth* (Backus and Chapian 1980) uses a Christian approach to challenge negative thinking and enhance healthy thought patterns that reduce anxiety and fear.

Interpersonal psychotherapy (IPT) is a psychodynamic approach that can help older persons with anxiety as well as depression. This technique emphasizes the importance of the therapeutic alliance, relationship between patient and therapist, and focuses on historical causes for present behaviors and feelings. In IPT, the patient's ongoing emotional experience both with the therapist and with other persons in his or her life is of particular importance. Reminiscence therapy, RT, can also help elders who are anxious by encouraging them to remember the past and share those memories either with a therapist or with others in a group therapy setting. The goal of RT is to re-experience old conflicts and rework them to a therapeutic resolution. These conflicts may indeed be underlying the elder's present anxieties.

ANXIETY AND FAITH

While Freud wrote much about the neurosis-producing effects of religion, there is no solid evidence from scientific research that the devoutly religious are more neurotic or anxious than those who are not religious. In fact, the opposite appears to be true. We found that the rate of anxiety disorder among younger adults who attended church once a week or more was only about one-half the rate of those who attended church less often (Koenig et al. 1993). A number of studies have also found that the devoutly religious experience less fear of death (Koenig 1995).

Why is this true, and how can clergy and religious caregivers use this information when counseling older adults who complain of fear and anxiety? The Scriptures contain many references to persons who were anxious or afraid but received comfort from God and were victorious over their circumstances. Take for example the following promises in Scripture: "You will keep in perfect peace him whose mind is steadfast, because he trusts in you" (Isa. 26:3, NIV); "But the fruit of the Spirit is love, joy, peace. . . ." (Gal. 5:22, NIV); "For God did not give us a spirit of fear, but a spirit of power, of love and of self-discipline" (2 Tim. 1:7, NIV; KJV uses, *a sound mind* in place of *self-discipline*).

Having elders memorize these verses and repeat them during times of anxiety or fear can effectively reduce symptoms. Studies have shown that repeating verses of religious scripture and saying repetitive prayers can reduce anxiety faster than the use of traditional psychotherapy and drug therapy alone (Azhart et al. 1994). For example, a middle-aged man had a phobia of crossing streets. Formal psychotherapy and medication was ineffective in relieving his phobia. Nevertheless, this man was able to overcome his fear by repeating Bible verses as he crossed the street. Group prayer and laying on of hands by clergy have also been known to relieve the symptoms of panic attacks. Some anxiety disorders, however, require multimodal therapy. Prayer, repeating religious scriptures, taking medication, and cognitive-behavioral therapy may all be required to effectively relieve symptoms in some elders with lifelong anxiety problems.

15

WHAT CAN BE DONE TO HELP OLDER PERSONS WITH CANCER OR TERMINAL ILLNESS?

"Even though I walk through the valley of the shadow of death, I will fear no evil, for you are with me; your rod and your staff, they comfort me."
—Psalm 23:4, NIV

Persons who are dying often need someone to talk to about what is happening to them. They need someone with whom to share their fears and questions, their hopes of a miracle, and their deep sorrow over leaving friends and loved ones behind. This is a very difficult area, one that requires a special calling from God. Many persons do not have this calling. Ministering to the dying may re-ignite deeply buried pains of long ago from losing a loved one. There are few areas of ministry, however, as important as helping persons approach that threshold between life on earth and life with God. It is at this time that people are most receptive to spiritual issues; it is here that only the really important things in life matter.

Surveys of persons who are dying have revealed information about their greatest needs. Older adults with cancer or other terminal illnesses do not so much fear the pain of their illness, other discomforts of dying, or even the prospect of death itself. Rather, their greatest fear is that they will die alone. Family members may be so upset by the dying of a loved one that they retreat. There may even be some attempts by family members and friends to distance themselves emotionally before the person dies in order to reduce the pain of eventual separation. Such withdrawal is a tragedy, for this is the very abandonment that the dying person fears the most.

Instead, the days, hours, and moments before death should be a time of reconciliation, a time of communicating forgiveness and a release from hurts inflicted in the past. It should be a time for expressing to the dying person how much his or her love and friendship has meant throughout the years and allowing the dying person to do the same for you. It is a time for listening and being present, not making idle chatter. This is a time of coming before God with the loved one in the last minutes of his or her life and placing the loved one's hand in the hand of Christ. Christ will accompany the loved one on the rest of his or her journey and will keep him or her safe until all are reunited once more someday when it is time to cross that threshold.

A clergyperson or a religious caregiver is the person that dying persons and their family members often look to for direction. They often do not know what to do or how to react. Pastoral counselors have the opportunity to help persons achieve a good death, one that will enrich the lives of those left behind, rather than leaving wounded people hurting and full of regrets. While pastoral counselors cannot (and should not try to) control what happens, they should be prepared to gently and carefully respond to needs as they arise.

DECISIONS ABOUT LIFE SUPPORT

When older adults are severely ill in the hospital or a nursing home, they or their family may approach pastoral counselors with questions about what they should do concerning cardiopulmonary resuscitation (CPR), ventilator support, feeding tubes, IVs and administration of antibiotics, and other interventions to provide life support. They may view the pastoral counselor as the one person who may provide objective, moral advice on what to do, particularly if they have little or no relationship with the doctors. This will likely make the pastoral counselor feel uncomfortable and even inadequate, but it is a role that he or she may need to assume in some cases.

In order to provide accurate and appropriate advice, pastoral counselors will need information about each of these procedures. CPR is what doctors and nurses do to patients if their heart and/or breathing stops suddenly; it involves external compressions of the chest (to get the heart pumping again) and mouth-to-mouth resuscitation (to circulate air into the lungs). The outcome of CPR when performed in the hospital on sick, elderly patients is not encouraging. Only 5% to 15% of such persons ever leave the hospital alive and, of those, 30% leave with poor mental functioning (Bedell et al. 1983).

Ventilator support is necessary when a person can no longer breathe on his or her own. The ventilator performs the function of the lungs. Persons usually have an endotracheal tube inserted, through the voice box into the main airway, that allows the regular inflation of both lungs. If the heart is beating, a person's body can be kept alive indefinitely using the ventilator, even when the brain is no longer functioning. Many complications can occur from ventilator support, including chronic lung infections and complications that result from confinement to bed, such as bed sores, bladder infections, and so forth.

Feeding tubes are used to deliver nutrition to a person who is either unable to eat or refuses to eat. These may be used in circumstances where the failure of nutritional support would result in the person's death. Feeding tubes may be inserted through the person's nose, down the esophagus, and into his or her stomach; alternatively, particularly when the tube may be needed a long time, it is surgically inserted directly into the patient's stomach through the abdominal wall. The need for a feeding tube often arises with Alzheimer's or dementia patients who refuse to eat or take their medication.

Intravenous lines, IVs, may be necessary to deliver fluids to someone who is dehydrated or needs special medications, such as antibiotics, to fight off infection. In persons with advanced dementia, the question often comes up about whether to treat dehydration and infection or to simply allow these illnesses to take their natural course.

CPR and other extraordinary means of life support are becoming a focus of concern in medicine because excessive uses of these procedures in the past dramatically ran up the cost of health care and kept persons alive who should have been allowed to die natural deaths. The sacredness of life takes on a whole new meaning as our technologies allow us to extend life almost indefinitely but at enormous cost to society, to the patient, and to his or her family. Until managed care arrived on the scene, the debate for patient autonomy held that persons should be allowed to refuse life-extending treatments and more recently, even be allowed to end their lives prematurely by suicide should they choose. Managed care, however, has added an interesting twist to the controversy. Instead of making more money when patients accept treatment, as it was in the past, hospitals and doctors now make more money when patients refuse treatments or commit suicide. The ethical debate has begun to turn around, now that patients and their families are having to fight much harder to get life-extending treatments rather than fighting to refuse them.

LIVING WILLS

Living wills, or advanced directives, are documents that express patients' preferences in terms of what types of medical care they wish to receive should they become terminal, incurable, or should they go into a persistent vegetative state, losing all brain functions. Living wills often specify whether or not the person wants CPR, ventilator support, IVs, feeding tubes, treatment of infections, transportation to the hospital when sick, and other medical procedures should he or she become severely ill and uncommunicative. Persons can revoke or make changes in a living will at any time. To complete a living will, an elder does not need to see an attorney. The person must, however, sign the document in front of witnesses, and it must be notarized by a notary public. Witnesses cannot be relatives or anyone who might benefit from the elder's health care decisions; witnesses are often persons who work at the bank where the elder does his or her business. A living will is not a legal document, and relatives may still sue the physician if they disagree with instructions in the living will that the physician followed.

In years past, the major purpose of living wills was to allow persons to refuse medical treatments, operating under the principle of patient autonomy noted above. Because it is now to their financial gain for hospitals to get patients to complete living wills, there has been a reexamination of these documents and the ethical concerns about their use (Callahan 1996).

Rather than complete a living will, it may be wiser for the elder to designate someone to make health care decisions on his or her behalf should the elder become incompetent. This is called a "durable health care power of attorney." The procedure for completing a durable power of attorney is the same as for a living will and does not require a lawyer. This is a legal document that immediately takes effect when the patient becomes incompetent or otherwise unable to make decisions on his or her own. It also applies more widely, rather than being restricted to terminal illness, incurable illness, or persistent vegetative state as living wills are in some states. A "durable power of attorney for financial decisions" works in the same way, but it is probably wise to involve a lawyer when drawing up this document. Any power of attorney can be changed or revoked at any time by the competent elder. For more information about end-of-life decision making, see *The American Geriatrics Society's Complete Guide to Aging and Health* (Williams 1995).

CONCLUSION

The aging process is characterized by heterogeneity. In other words, no two persons age exactly alike. As persons get older, they tend to differ more and more from each other. As Thomas Merton observed, "individuality is no imperfection" in the providence of God. In fact, our Creator appears to celebrate difference and variety. It is important that such "individuality" and uniqueness be appreciated by those ministering to older adults.

Studies tell us that religious beliefs often become more important to us as we age. A central goal of this book has been to share practical information to help enhance ministry to the social, mental, and physical needs of seniors, as they increasingly rely upon the support and counsel of the community of faith. It has been our aim to focus on priority areas clergy and religious caregivers have pointed out to us. As we have emphasized, a senior's mental and physical well-being is often deeply affected by the state of their spiritual health. Those of us in ministry have powerful resources at our disposal to promote the well-being of our aging brothers and sisters.

We end with words penned by Martin Luther in 1524, when he was a young man of 41 years. These words of faith taken from his hymn titled, "We Now Implore God the Holy Ghost," remind us of the source of all our health and hope:

> Thou sacred Love, grace on us bestow,
> Set our hearts with heavenly fire aglow
> That with hearts united we love each other.
> Of one mind, in peace with every brother.
> Lord have mercy!

Thou highest Comfort in every need,
Grant that neither shame nor death we heed
That even then our courage may never fail us
When the foe shall accuse and assail us.
Lord have mercy!

REFERENCES

American Association of Retired Persons. 1986. *A profile of older persons: 1986.* Washington, D.C.: American Association of Retired Persons.

Azhart, M. A., S. L. Varma, and A. S. Dharap. 1994. Religious psychotherapy in anxiety disorder patients. *Acta Psychiatrica Scandinavica* 90:1–3.

Backus, W., and M. Chapian. 1980. *Telling yourself the truth.* Bethany House Publishers: Minneapolis.

Bedell, S. E., T. L. Delbanco, E. F. Cook, and F. H. Epstein. 1983. Survival after cardiopulmonary resuscitation in the hospital. *New England Journal of Medicine* 309:569–76.

Burns, D. D. 1980. *Feeling good: The new mood therapy.* New York: The New American Library.

Callahan, D. 1996. Controlling the costs of health care for the elderly—fair means and foul. *New England Journal of Medicine* 335:744–46.

Cantor, M. 1983. Strain among caregivers: A study of experience in the United States. *Gerontologist* 23:597–604.

Dean, M. 1990. Grey growth. *Lancet* 335:1330–1331

Gallup, G. H. 1992. *Attitude and incidence of suicide among the elderly.* Princeton, N.J.: The Gallup Organization, Inc.

Guralnik, J. M., A. Z. LaCroix, D. F. Everett, and M. G. Kovar. 1995. Aging in the eighties: The prevalence of comorbidity and its association with disability. *Advance Data* (from Vital and Health Statistics of the National Center for Health Statistics), number 170:1–8.

Havlik, R. J., B. M. Liu, M. G. Kovar, R. Suzman, J. J. Feldman, T. Harris, and J. Van Nostrand. 1987. Health statistics on older persons: United States, 1986. *Vital Health Statistics* ser. 3, 25:1–157.

Jamison, E. 1991. *World population profile: 1991 (U.S. Bureau of the Census, report WP/91)*. Washington, D.C.: U.S. Government Printing Office.

Kane, R. L., D. M. Radosevich, and J. W. Vaupel. 1990. Compression of morbidity: Issues and irrelevancies. In *Improving the Health of Older People: A World View*. Edited by R. Kane, J. Evans, and D. MacFayden. 30–49. Oxford, England: Oxford University Press.

Kemper, P., and C. Murtaugh. 1991. Lifetime use of nursing home care. *New England Journal of Medicine* 324:595–600.

Koenig, H. G. 1995. *Research on religion and aging*. Westport, Conn.: Greenwood Press.

———. 1997. *Is religion good for your health?* Binghamton, N.Y.: Haworth Press.

Koenig, H. G., H. J. Cohen, D. G. Blazer, C. Pieper, K. G. Meador, F. Shelp, V. Goli, and R. DiPasquale. 1992. Religious coping and depression in elderly hospitalized medically ill men. *American Journal of Psychiatry* 149:1693–1700.

Koenig, H. G., S. Ford, L. K. George, D. G. Blazer, and K. G. Meador. 1993. Religion and anxiety disorder: An examination and comparison of associations in young, middle-aged, and elderly adults. *Journal of Anxiety Disorders* 7:321–42.

Koenig, H. G., L. K. George, and B. L. Peterson. 1998. Religiosity and remission from depression in medically ill older patients. *American Journal of Psychiatry* 155:536–42.

Koenig, H. G., L. K. George, and R. Schneider. 1994. Mental health care for older adults in the year 2020: A dangerous and avoided topic. *Gerontologist* 34:674–79.

Koenig, H. G., T. Lamar, and B. Lamar. 1997. *A gospel for the mature years: Finding fulfillment by knowing and using our gifts*. Binghamton, N.Y.: Haworth Press.

Koenig, H. G., and A. J. Weaver. 1997. *Counseling older adults and their families: A handbook for pastors and religious caregivers*. Nashville: Abingdon Press.

Kunkel, S. R., and R. A. Applebaum. 1992. Estimating the prevalence of long-term disability for an aging society. *Journal of Gerontology (Social Sciences)* 47:253–60.

Mace, N. L., and P. V. Rabins. 1981. *The 36-hour day: A family guide to caring for persons with Alzheimer's disease, related dementing illnesses, and memory loss in later life.* Baltimore: Johns Hopkins University Press.

Mulligan, M. A., and R. Bennett. 1977. Assessment of mental health and social problems during multiple friendly visits: The development and evaluation of a friendly visit program for the isolated elderly. *International Journal of Aging and Human Development* 8:43–65.

Myers, G. 1990. Demography of aging. In *Handbook of Aging and the Social Sciences,* 3d ed. Edited by R. Binstock and L. George. San Diego: Academic Press, 19–44.

National Center for Health Statistics. 1993. Advance report of final mortality statistics, 1991. Vol. 42 of *Monthly Vital Statistics Report,* no. 2, suppl. Hyattsville, Md.: Public Health Service.

National Institutes of Health. 1991. Diagnosis and treatment of depression in late life. Vol. 9 of *Consensus Development Conference Statement,* no. 3.

N.C. Division of Aging. 1995. *A North Carolina caregiver's handbook.* N.C. Department of Human Resources, Division of Aging.

Preston, J. D. 1996. *You can beat depression: A guide to prevention and recovery.* San Luis Obispo, Calif.: Impact Publishers.

Propst, L. R., R. Ostrom, P. Watkins, T. Dean, and D. Mashburn. 1992. Comparative efficacy of religious and nonreligious cognitive-behavioral therapy for the treatment of clinical depression in religious individuals. *Journal of Consulting and Clinical Psychology* 60:94–103.

Rabins, P. V., M. D. Fitting, J. Eastham, and J. Zabora. 1990. Emotional adaptation over time in care-givers for chronically ill elderly people. *Age and Aging* 19:185–90.

Reisberg, B. 1996. Alzheimer's disease. In *Comprehensive Review of Geriatric Psychiatry—II.* Edited by J. Sadavoy, L. W. Lazarus, L. F. Jarvik, and G. T. Grossberg. Washington, D.C.: American Psychiatric Press.

Saluter, A. F. 1992. Marital status and living arrangements: March 1991. *U.S. Bureau of the Census, Current Population Reports,* ser. P-20, no. 461. Washington, D.C.: U.S. Government Printing Office.

Sullender, S. R. 1985. *Losses in later life: A new way of walking with God.* New York: Paulist Press.

Tauber, C. 1992. Sixty-five plus in America. *U.S. Bureau of the Census, Current Population Reports. Special Studies,* P23–178. Washington, D.C.: U.S. Government Printing Office.

Weaver, A. J. 1993. Depression, what clergy need to know. *Currents in Theology and Mission* 20(1): 5–16.

———. 1995. Has there been a failure to prepare and support parish-based clergy in their role as front-line community mental health workers?: A review. *The Journal of Pastoral Care* 49:129–49.

Weaver, A. J., and H. G. Koenig. 1996. Elderly suicide, mental health professionals and the clergy: A need for collaboration, training and research. *Death Studies* 20(5):495–508.

Weaver, A. J., H. G. Koenig , and J. Preston. 1996. Elderly suicide prevention: What pastors need to know. *The Quarterly Review* (summer), 151–67.

Weaver, A. J., H. G. Koenig, and P. Roe, ed. 1998. *Reflections on aging and spiritual growth.* Nashville: Abingdon Press.

Williams, M. E. 1995. *The American Geriatrics Society's complete guide to aging and health.* New York: Harmony Books.